OFF THE HOOK

OFF THE HOOK

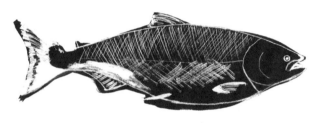

THE ESSENTIAL WEST COAST
SEAFOOD RECIPES

By DL Acken and Aurelia Louvet

TOUCHWOOD EDITIONS

To my dad, Peter,
who taught me to love the sea and all that it provides,
and my mum, Nicole,
who always made the kitchen the heart of our home.
—*Danielle [DL] Acken*

To my husband, François,
who drives my passion for food;
my father, Jean-Pierre, who ignited it;
and my grandmother, Mamie Susanne,
whose kitchen produced some of
my most cherished childhood memories.
—*Aurelia Louvet*

CONTENTS

INTRODUCTION

Growing up here on the West Coast, I spent a lot of my early days out on the water with my father, catching and later cooking the freshest of fish. Often we'd be out on the boat before the sun rose, accompanying the commercial boats out to the fishing grounds, and we'd return before breakfast with a day's catch in our hold. Even today, the smell of fire-roasted salmon brings with it a wave of nostalgia that leaves my mouth watering and my belly rumbling for the deliciousness that follows. From the seasonal spot prawns to a rich and robust halibut fillet to our wild Pacific salmon, these foods have defined my culinary upbringing and remain a huge part of the cooking I do at home today. Aurelia, my co-author and an incredibly talented food stylist, grew up internationally and is a recent transplant to this corner of the world, but her passion for beautiful, fresh food found instant purchase here, and her recipes are as influenced by innovative West Coast flavours as they are by classic French cooking techniques.

So what are essential West Coast seafood recipes? To Aurelia and me, they are the everyday, easy, and accessible dishes that seafood lovers tend to enjoy, and moreover, most of these are adaptable to suit all palates—even those of picky children. English Style Beer-Battered Lingcod is a direct approximation of what my dad always made whenever we were lucky enough to pull up a big one, and it was my absolute favourite supper as a young child.

Both Aurelia and I have a love of all things spicy and as such, you'll often find the inclusion of a bit of heat, but always with a variation that allows for a little less punch if desired. You'll also find a heavy emphasis on Asian ingredients, as they heavily influence the culinary scene here in BC, but again, we've given options to allow different herbs and botanicals to come through if that is more to your liking. Our West Coast versions of classic East Coast dishes are true representations of the flavours that surround us, and they represent the best of what's available here in our home waters.

As a caterer-turned-food photographer, I'm accustomed to cooking for a crowd, but we've adjusted some of the most popular party dishes down to family-sized portions for everyday use. That being said, we're sure that many of our recipes will become instant favourites in your house and your go-to choices when guests come around. The Dungeness Crab Cakes can easily be doubled and made in miniature for easy appetizers, as can the Shrimp Balls and the Coconut Prawns, perfect for the holiday season or summer evenings with friends.

From juicy line-caught fish favourites to delicious shellfish classics, our hope is that you'll take licence with the dishes here and make them your own, so that they truly become your family's Essential West Coast Seafood Recipes, ones you come back to again and again. Happy cooking!

A SEAFOOD LOVER'S PANTRY

The recipes in this book are, to us, the quintessential collection that every West Coast seafood lover needs to have on hand, especially for fresh, uncomplicated yet delicious go-to meals. You'll find that we've kept the ingredients to a minimum where possible, allowing the freshness of the seafood in each dish to shine through. Having a few staples at home will help make whipping up these recipes even easier. We've also given you our homemade versions of all the classic sauces, but in a pinch, good-quality store-bought ones will do.

Produce
Lemons
Limes
Fresh thyme
Fresh cilantro
Fresh parsley
Fresh dill
Garlic

Spices
Red pepper flakes
Bay leaves
Black peppercorns
Flake sea salt for finishing
Chipotle powder
Smoked paprika

Equipment
Parchment paper
Candy/Deep-fry thermometer
Oyster shucker
Large stock pot

Condiments and Common Ingredients
Sriracha
Sambal oelek
Mirin
Soy sauce
Chipotle peppers (canned)
Worcestershire sauce
Olive oil
Thai curry paste
Coconut milk
Mayonnaise
Panko bread crumbs
Chickpea flour
Dark ale
Capers
Eggs

For the
LOVE
of
FINS

I have a passion for all things fin-y! Whether it's a perfectly glazed sablefish fillet, a cedar-planked barbecued salmon, or half a dozen of Fanny Bay's most beautiful oysters on the half shell, there's nothing like bringing the freshness of our West Coast waters to the dinner table. Of course, with a love of the ocean and all that it provides comes a deep sense of responsibility when choosing what to eat and sourcing it. It's no secret that our environment is in deep need of sustainable practices, and none of our delicate coastal ecosystems seems more in need of our attention than the waters that surround us. For home cooks, this can seem like a daunting task, but it needn't be. To find the freshest, best-fished seafood, simply make friends with your fishmonger: find out how a fish was caught, where it's from, how long it's been frozen, etc. Many methods of fishing raise concerns about large amounts of wasted bycatch (fish unintentionally caught in nets), and ocean-bottom environmental damage is a growing problem, but making good choices or asking a responsible fishmonger should alleviate your concerns and keep you feeling good about the food choices you're making. The Ocean Wise website (seafood.ocean.org) is a vast resource for those who want to look even further into sustainability and good fishing practices.

Some people are daunted by the thought of preparing fish to eat, but a good fishmonger is also your best friend when it comes to getting your fish ready to cook. If you're not completely confident in your technical or knife skills when it comes to seafood, you can always ask them to pin-bone a fillet of salmon or skin a halibut for you, thus making your time in the kitchen shorter, easier, and ultimately more enjoyable.

Of course, the key to cooking great fish is making sure it's as fresh as possible, whether that means buying it straight off the boat or flash-frozen at sea. Here on the West Coast, we have access to some of the most beautiful fish in the world and, with a healthy fishing industry, most are fresh and available from local merchants during their season in a staggering variety. Certain species, such as halibut and sablefish, offer a meat that stands up well to rich sauces and strong marinades or glazes, while those in the rockfish family—such as cod and snapper—have a delicate texture, perfect for soups, curries, and even a good fry. Some fish, including the tiny smelt and the king of them all, the wild Pacific salmon, need little more than a splash of lemon juice and fresh herbs to bring their flavours to perfection, and they do just as well in a frying pan as they do over an open fire.

Whatever fish is on your menu, be sure it smells of nothing more than a slightly salty sea—your nose will always tell you exactly how fresh your fish is.

Salmon
* * *

Smoked Salmon Devilled Eggs **20**

Candied Salmon Cucumber Cups **22**

Smoked Salmon Terrine with Grilled Crostini **24**

Candied Salmon Salad with
Maple-Glazed Hazelnuts and Chèvre **26**

Smoked Salmon, Asparagus,
and Chèvre Breakfast Strata **27**

Beet-Cured Gravlax with Easy Apple Pickle **28**

Salmon Burger with Sriracha Aioli **30**

Salmon Wellington **32**

Maple Black Pepper Cedar Plank Salmon **33**

Fire-Roasted Whole Pacific Salmon **34**

Tuna
* * *

Tuna Poke Bowl **40**

Tuna Tartare **42**

Nouveau Niçoise Salad **44**

Sesame-Crusted Tuna
with Wasabi Mashed Potatoes **45**

Halibut
* * *

Pacific Seafood Chowder **48**

Mojito-Glazed Grilled Halibut **50**

Potato-Wrapped Halibut **51**

West Coast Fish Pie **52**

*Pan-Seared Halibut Cheeks with
Citrus Brown Butter Sauce* **54**

Sablefish
* * *

Miso Ginger Glazed Sablefish **58**

Tomato Turmeric Grilled Sablefish **60**

Cod
* * *

*Blackened Cod Tacos with
Chipotle Peach Salsa and Slaw* **64**

Cod en Papillote with Herb Butter **66**

English-Style Beer-Battered Lingcod **68**

Rockfish & Smelt
* * *

Curried Rockfish Hot Pot **72**

*Grilled Whole Smelt with
Sweet Chili Lemon Sauce* **74**

SALMON

Flavourful, versatile, and sought-after, salmon truly is the king of these Pacific waters. The depth of flavour and wide variety of culinary uses make it an extremely versatile and sought-after fish. It's also one of our favourites to prepare and eat—even kids love it! Of course, with this popularity comes a need for extreme caution within the salmon fishing industry; as such, measures are currently being taken to preserve stocks and implement sustainable fishing practices. There are many methods of catching salmon, and most fishing companies working in our waters live up to Canada's strict guidelines when it comes to bycatch and environmental impact.

For us, it comes down to where the fish was caught and by who. We like to know that the fisherfolk we're buying from are working in waters with large numbers and that they're using every means possible to preserve the population. A limited number of freshwater closed-containment coho farms have popped up; they're worth looking into because they offer a low environmental impact, but we feel that wild, well-caught salmon from areas where the numbers are high are your best bet for conscious eating.

Salmon is easy to prepare: a good fishmonger can cut you perfect fillets (side-cut meat) or steaks (full cross-sections including the spine) and will usually be happy to pin-bone the fillets for you. Pin bones are those small, rib-like bones that poke out from the flesh—they can be a choking hazard and unpleasant to pick out of your teeth, so removing them is always preferable. If you need to remove them at home, a pair of needle-nose pliers will pull them out quite easily: just run your hand along the fillet to feel for the bones, then give a gentle tug with the pliers to free them from the flesh.

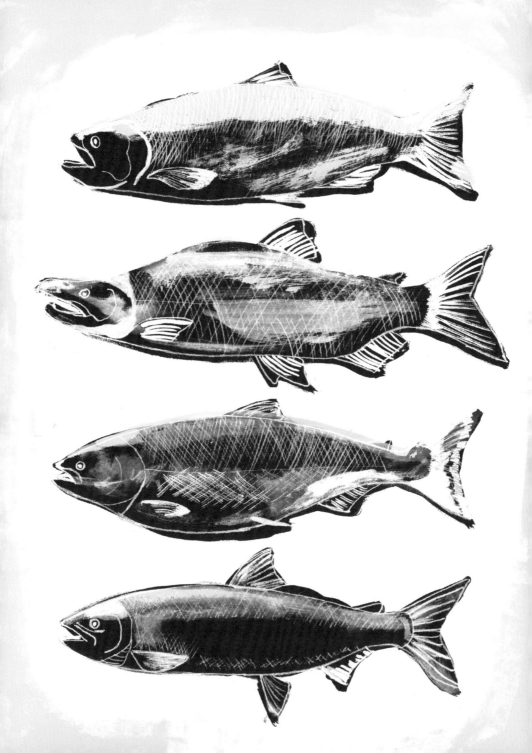

Smoked Salmon Devilled Eggs

This recipe works beautifully with regular hard-boiled eggs, but if you have the time, the beet-pickled version is extremely pretty. The recipe doubles well if needed.

Add the vinegar, sea salt, sugar, water, and beet slices to a medium pot. Simmer until the beets are tender, about 30 minutes. Drain, reserving the brine.

Fill a medium pot with water and place the eggs inside. Cover and bring to a boil. Turn off heat and let stand for 10 minutes. Drain and peel the eggs.

Place the eggs in a glass jar and fill with the beet brine. Refrigerate for at least 3 hours.

Remove the eggs from the brine and cut them in half lengthwise. Remove the yolks. Place the yolks, the smoked salmon, goat cheese, sour cream, and chives in a medium bowl and using a hand mixer, or a fork if mixing by hand, blend together until smooth. Place mixture in a piping bag and pipe it back into the egg-white halves. Cover loosely with plastic wrap and refrigerate for 30 minutes. To serve, place the eggs on a platter and top with the salmon roe.

Serves 8 to 10

2 cups (500 mL) white
   vinegar
1 Tbsp (15 mL) sea salt
2 Tbsp (30 mL) sugar
½ cup (125 mL) water
1 medium beet, peeled and
   sliced ½-inch thick
8 eggs
4 oz (115 g) smoked salmon,
   finely chopped
2 oz (60 g) goat cheese,
   softened
⅓ cup (80 mL) sour cream
1 Tbsp (15 mL) finely
   chopped chives
¼ cup (60 mL) salmon roe

Candied Salmon Cucumber Cups

You can easily enhance the flavour of these pretty little hors d'oeuvres by adding a touch of maple syrup, sriracha, or any type of botanical herbs you enjoy to the mixture before pulsing. Feeding a crowd? The recipe will easily double, triple, or more.

Wash the cucumbers and then slice each into 24 half-inch (1 cm) thick rounds. Using a melon baller or the tip of a teaspoon, scoop out the centre of each round to create a small indentation—do not go all the way through the slice.

Place the cream cheese and about 5 oz (140 g) of the candied salmon in a food processor. Pulse until the mixture is fairly smooth. Using a piping bag or dropping with a teaspoon, fill the indentation of each cucumber round and top with a small sliver of the reserved candied salmon. Can be stored in the refrigerator for up to 30 minutes. Sprinkle with flake sea salt and serve chilled.

Makes 2 dozen

2 long English cucumbers
1 cup (250 mL) cream cheese
6 oz (170 g) candied salmon, divided
Flake sea salt to finish

Smoked Salmon Terrine
with Grilled Crostini

We've used classic lox for this recipe, but candied or super dry smoked salmon will work equally well and will impart its own unique flavours into the final terrine. This recipe would also work nicely with a delicate whitefish, so if you have some ends of smoked cod or even some smoked trout, this is a good opportunity to use them up.

Combine smoked salmon, cream cheese, heavy cream, lemon zest, dill, capers, and black pepper in a food processor. Blend until smooth.

Transfer to 6 to 8 medium wide-mouthed Mason jars or ramekins and cover. Chill 6 to 8 hours or overnight.

Just before serving, preheat your oven's broiler. Arrange the sliced baguette on a baking sheet in a single layer. Brush both sides of the pieces with olive oil. Broil for 5 minutes or until golden brown. Serve grilled crostini with the chilled terrine and freshly cut lemon slices.

Serves 6 to 8

20 oz (600 g) smoked salmon lox
18 oz (500 g) cream cheese, softened
¼ cup (60 mL) heavy cream
1 Tbsp (15 mL) freshly grated lemon zest
½ cup (125 mL) chopped fresh dill
2 Tbsp (30 mL) capers
¼ tsp (1 mL) freshly cracked black pepper
1 baguette, cut at an angle into ½-inch-thick slices
¼ cup (60 mL) olive oil
1 lemon, sliced for serving

Candied Salmon Salad with Maple-Glazed Hazelnuts and Chèvre

We have several hazelnut farms here on the West Coast and the meatiness of these nuts goes well with the sweet candied salmon, but using the same method with pecans, walnuts, almonds, or whatever you have on hand will work just as well. Feel free to replace the champagne vinegar with red wine vinegar, white wine vinegar, sherry vinegar, or even balsamic vinegar. What matters most is the proportion of acid to oil: so long as the proportions stay the same, it doesn't matter which vinegar you choose.

Preheat the oven to 375°F (190°C). In a bowl, toss the hazelnuts with the maple syrup. Pour the coated nuts out onto a parchment-lined baking sheet and bake for 7 to 10 minutes or until the glaze begins to bubble. Remove the sheet from the oven and let cool completely.

Place the champagne vinegar, Dijon mustard, and honey in a small mixing bowl, stirring to combine. While whisking constantly, slowly drizzle in the olive oil. Continue whisking until all the ingredients have combined into a thick vinaigrette dressing. Season with sea salt and freshly cracked black pepper to taste.

Place the greens in a large salad bowl and toss with the vinaigrette. Divide the greens among 4 plates and arrange the salmon, chèvre, and hazelnuts on top. Serve immediately.

Serves 4

1 cup (250 mL) raw hazelnuts

2 Tbsp (30 mL) maple syrup

1 Tbsp (15 mL) champagne vinegar

½ tsp (2.5 mL) Dijon mustard

½ tsp (2.5 mL) honey

1½ Tbsp (23 mL) extra virgin olive oil

Sea salt and freshly cracked black pepper to taste

6 cups (1.5 L) mixed salad greens

6 oz (170 g) candied salmon nuggets, broken into bite-sized pieces

6 oz (170 g) chèvre, crumbled

Smoked Salmon, Asparagus, and Chèvre Breakfast Strata

The bare bones of this recipe are the foundation of every strata (eggs, milk, bread) and basically create a savoury bread pudding. Feel free to get creative with the flavours, seasonings, and other ingredients. Strata is best when it's left to sit for at least 3 to 4 hours, preferably overnight; make one the night before and enjoy it as a no-fuss breakfast the next day.

Grease a 9 × 13-inch (3 L) glass baking dish. In a medium-sized bowl, whisk the eggs and milk together until blended well. Add the Dijon mustard, dill, capers, salt, and pepper and mix them to combine.

In a large bowl, mix together the bread, salmon, chèvre, asparagus, and red onion. Pour the egg and milk mixture over the dry-ingredient mixture and toss to combine evenly. Then pour this mixture into the glass baking dish, being sure to distribute it fairly evenly. Cover with plastic wrap or a lid and place in the refrigerator for at least 1 hour and as long as overnight.

Preheat the oven to 350°F (180°C). Uncover the baking dish and place on the middle rack. Bake for 1 hour or until the strata becomes golden and set in the centre—it should not jiggle when gently shaken. Let it cool for 5 to 10 minutes before cutting. Serve with crème fraîche or Dill Crema (page 150).

Serves 6 to 8

Egg and Milk Mixture
10 eggs
3 cups (750 mL) whole milk
1 Tbsp (15 mL) Dijon mustard
2 Tbsp (30 mL) chopped fresh dill
2 Tbsp (30 mL) drained capers
Pinch of sea salt
Pinch of freshly ground black pepper

Dry Ingredients
1 medium sized loaf of bread, cubed
6 oz (170 g) thinly sliced smoked salmon cut into 1-inch (2.5 cm) pieces
1 cup (250 mL) crumbled fresh chèvre
8 to 10 stalks of asparagus, bottoms trimmed and cut into 1-inch pieces
½ cup (125 mL) thinly sliced red onion

Beet-Cured Gravlax
with Easy Apple Pickle

This salmon is delicious on bagels with cream cheese and is a nice addition to salads or used in the Smoked Salmon, Asparagus, and Chèvre Breakfast Strata (page 27). The Apple Pickle is delicious with myriad other foods as well. Try it on a salad with candied salmon, or even as a side to chicken or pork.

Combine the first 6 ingredients in a small bowl. Set aside.

Place the salmon on a piece of parchment paper large enough to cover it. Crust the entire piece of fish with the sea salt and sugar mixture. Then, coat it with the grated beets. Fold the parchment paper around it and wrap tightly in plastic wrap. In the fridge, place the wrapped fish between two baking sheets and weigh down the top with a cast-iron pan or a number of cans. Keep it like this in the fridge for two days.

To make the apple pickle, slice the apples into matchsticks. Place in a wide-mouth Mason jar. Add vinegar, sugar, sea salt, orange zest, and ginger. Refrigerate for at least 30 minutes.

Take the salmon out of the fridge and remove the plastic and parchment paper. Pour off any liquid and wipe off the excess cure. Do not rinse the fish.

Using a sharp knife, cut the salmon into very thin slices. Use immediately or refrigerate to keep cold until ready to serve.

Serves 6 to 8

Crust
1 tsp (5 mL) freshly grated
   lemon zest
2 dried juniper berries,
   ground
2 Tbsp (30 mL) finely
   chopped dill
1 tsp (5 mL) liquid smoke
6 Tbsp (90 mL) coarse
   sea salt
2 Tbsp (30 mL) sugar

1 lb (450 g) coho or wild
   sockeye salmon
2 large purple beets,
   peeled and grated

Apple Pickle
2 medium apples, cored
1 cup (250 mL) vinegar
2 Tbsp (30 mL) sugar
1 Tbsp (15 mL) coarse sea salt
1 Tbsp (15 mL) orange zest
1 Tbsp (15 mL) peeled,
   finely chopped ginger

Salmon Burger with Sriracha Aioli

If you're looking for a gluten-free version of this burger, 2 Tbsp (30 mL) chickpea or coconut flour can be substituted for the panko. If you have neither on hand, any gluten-free binding flour will work. Not a fan of cilantro? Replace it with finely chopped fresh dill and the ginger with Dijon mustard. Top with Dill Crema (page 150).

Cut the salmon into chunks and pulse in a food processor until loosely chopped. Add the cilantro, green onion, ginger, sea salt, and pepper, then pulse twice, until just combined. Add the lime zest and juice, sambal oelek, panko, and mayonnaise and pulse again briefly.

Heat the olive oil in a skillet over medium-high heat. Shape the salmon mixture into 4 × 4-inch (10 × 10 cm) patties approximately 1 inch (2½ cm) thick. Fry until golden brown on both sides, about 4 minutes per side. Place on a plate lined with paper towels and keep warm in the oven until serving.

Slice the buns in half and toast lightly. Spread 1 Tbsp (15 mL) Sriracha Aioli on each bun half, fill with burger, lettuce, tomato, and pickle. Serve warm.

Serves 4

1 lb (450 g) salmon fillets
¼ cup (60 mL) finely chopped fresh cilantro
1 green onion, finely chopped
½ inch (1¼ cm) piece of fresh ginger, peeled and grated
2 tsp (10 mL) sea salt
1 tsp (5 mL) freshly cracked black pepper
1 tsp (5 mL) lime zest
1 Tbsp (15 mL) freshly squeezed lime juice
1 tsp (5 mL) sambal oelek or other hot sauce
¼ cup (60 mL) panko-style bread crumbs
⅓ cup (80 mL) mayonnaise
6 Tbsp (90 mL) olive oil
4 hearty kaiser-style buns
½ cup (125 mL) Sriracha Aioli (see page 149)
Lettuce, tomato, pickle

Salmon Wellington

The cream cheese mixture in this recipe can have any flavour profile you like. Here, we've done a classic spinach and dill, but you can swap out the dill for sun-dried tomatoes, olive tapenade, citrus and tarragon, or even something spicy like red pepper flakes and roasted red pepper.

Season the salmon with salt and pepper to taste. Let rest outside the fridge and come up to room temperature.

In a nonstick pan, heat the butter and shallot over medium heat, stirring occasionally; continue until the shallot is translucent. Add the garlic and stir another 30 seconds. Add the white wine and spinach, then sauté over medium heat, stirring occasionally, until the liquid has reduced by half. Add the cream cheese; heat through and stir to combine. Remove the pan from the heat and add the dill and asiago. Stir to combine well. Set aside.

Preheat the oven to 400°F (200°C).

On a lightly floured surface, roll out the 2 sheets of puff pastry and cut them in half to create 4 pieces. Each piece should provide a 2-inch (5 cm) edge around each salmon fillet. Spread a line of the cream cheese mixture across the middle of each piece of puff pastry and place a fillet (skinless side connecting with the mixture) on top.

Beat the egg with water in a small bowl, then lightly brush it onto the edges of each puff pastry piece.

Fold the pastry up, over, and around the fillets starting with the long sides and then folding in the short sides, much as you would wrap a present. Place each package on a parchment-lined baking sheet with the seam side down. You can use a knife to score a design on the top—try 3 to 4 diagonal slashes, a cross-hatch pattern, or 3 to 4 chevrons. Brush the top of each Wellington with the egg wash. Bake 20 to 25 minutes or until the pastry is puffed and golden brown. Let rest at least 5 minutes before serving.

Serves 4

4 × 6 oz (170 g) salmon
    fillets
Sea salt and freshly
    ground pepper to taste
3 Tbsp (45 mL) butter
1 shallot, chopped
2 garlic cloves, minced
¼ cup (60 mL) white wine
5 oz (140 g) fresh baby
    spinach
3 oz (85 g) cream cheese
2 Tbsp (30 mL) finely
    chopped fresh dill
¼ cup (60 mL) grated
    asiago cheese
1 lb (450 g) package
    of puff pastry
1 egg
1 tsp (5 mL) water

Maple Black Pepper Cedar Plank Salmon

If you don't have access to a cedar roasting plank, the salmon can be cooked directly on the grill at a lower temperature. Place on the grill, skin side down, for approximately 15 to 20 minutes—the skin will crisp and the salmon will be just cooked through when done.

Immerse an 18 to 20 inch (46 to 50 cm) cedar plank in water for at least 2 hours. If using a charcoal grill, heat the coals until they are glowing white; with a gas grill, heat to medium high.

In a small bowl, combine the maple syrup, mustard, black pepper, lemon zest, and lemon juice. Place the salmon in a roasting dish or other shallow pan and pour the marinade over top. Marinate 30 minutes to 2 hours.

Remove the salmon from the pan and place on the saturated cedar plank, skin side down. Season lightly with flake sea salt. Spoon the marinade from the pan over the salmon, covering it, and place the plank directly on the grill.

Cover the grill with the lid and cook for approximately 15 minutes or until the salmon is cooked through and the edges have begun to crisp. Remove the plank from the heat and let the salmon rest for 8 to 10 minutes. Serve with Dill Crema or Chipotle Peach Salsa.

Serves 6 to 8

3 Tbsp (45 mL) pure maple syrup

2 Tbsp (30 mL) grainy mustard

2 tsp (10 mL) freshly cracked black pepper

1 Tbsp (15 mL) freshly grated lemon zest

1 Tbsp (15 mL) freshly squeezed lemon juice

2 lb (900 g) salmon fillet with skin

½ tsp (2.5 mL) flake sea salt, sel de mer, or other similar salt

Dill Crema (page 150) or Chipotle Peach Salsa (page 64)

Fire-Roasted Whole Pacific Salmon

This is the way Danielle's father always cooked salmon when she was a child, and it's still her favourite way to eat it. The fish will take on the flavours of whatever it's stuffed with, so feel free to experiment: orange and fennel are a nice combination, as are tarragon and shallot.

Heat a charcoal grill until coals are glowing white. If using a gas grill, heat over medium-high heat.

Open the salmon and spread the butter over the inside. Squeeze the juice of one lemon over the inside and layer the lemon slices along both sides of the fish. Sprinkle the dill, green onion, and minced garlic over the inside. Season the inside of the fish with the salt and pepper. Seal the fish by running the toothpicks through the outer edge of the belly, effectively sewing the edges together.

Place the fish directly on the grill and close the lid. Cook approximately 10 to 15 minutes per side or until the internal temperature reaches 140°F (60°C) and the flesh flakes away from the bones easily.

Using a sharp knife, slice the flesh from the bone. Serve with Dill Crema.

Serves 8 to 10

Approx. 10 lb (4.5 kg) whole salmon, insides removed, head and tail attached

¼ cup (60 mL) butter, softened

1 lemon for juicing

1 lemon cut into thin slices

½ cup (125 mL) chopped fresh dill

½ cup (125 mL) chopped green onion

1 small garlic clove, minced

Sea salt and freshly cracked pepper to taste

10 toothpicks, soaked in water for at least 30 minutes

Dill Crema (page 150)

TUNA

If you haven't tried fresh, wild albacore tuna, you've been missing out on one of the greatest fish roaming these Pacific waters. Tuna are highly migratory and as such can be sustainably fished by responsible fisherfolk. Ask your local fishmonger for recommendations on well-sourced varieties and they'll point you in the right direction.

Unless it comes from a can, tuna is best served raw or very rare—it just melts in your mouth and the flavour is light and fresh. Be sure to source "sushi grade" tuna, meaning tuna that is of the highest quality and is considered relatively safe to eat when uncooked. You need to do little to tuna of this quality: a splash of citrus, a dash of sesame oil, or a quick sear in a very hot pan, and you pretty much have seafood perfection.

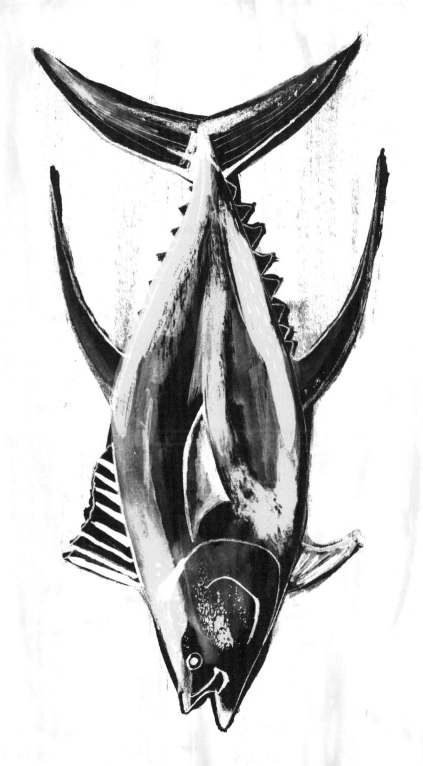

Tuna Poke Bowl

This dish is basically a salad, and thus any fresh vegetables will act as great accompaniments to the soft richness of the tuna. Try blanched asparagus, green beans, or even crispy, fresh, sautéed corn kernels when in season. When choosing your rice, any type will do, but we prefer either a long-grain basmati or a hearty brown variety to add another level of texture to the dish.

In a medium bowl, mix together soy sauce, rice vinegar, sesame oil, sugar, 1 tsp of sesame seeds, freshly cracked black pepper, and scallions. Toss the fish in the mixture and chill in the fridge 5 to 10 minutes.

Cut the avocado into pieces approximately the same size as the tuna cubes. Remove the tuna from the fridge and gently fold the avocado into the mixture.

To serve, place rice in small bowls and top with tuna mixture, carrot, snap peas, and radishes. Garnish with remaining sesame seeds.

Serves 2 to 4

2 Tbsp (30 mL) soy sauce
1 tsp (5 mL) rice vinegar
1 tsp (5 mL) toasted sesame oil
½ tsp (2.5 mL) coconut sugar (can substitute brown sugar)
2 tsp (10 mL) sesame seeds, divided
½ tsp (2.5 mL) freshly cracked black pepper
2 scallions, thinly sliced
1 lb (450 g) sushi-grade ahi tuna, cubed
1 avocado, pitted and cubed
2 cups (500 mL) cooked rice, any type
1 medium carrot, grated
8 snap peas, thinly sliced
4 radishes, quartered

Tuna Tartare

You can substitute sushi-grade salmon for the tuna in this recipe, or use a combination of tuna and salmon—very West Coast!

In a skillet, toast the sesame seeds over medium-low heat for 3 to 5 minutes, until golden. Remove from heat and place in a bowl.

In a large bowl, combine the tuna, ginger, soy sauce, lime juice, jalapeño, sesame oil, and chives.

To serve, divide the tuna and garnish with the toasted sesame seeds.

Serves 2 to 4

2 tsp (10 mL) sesame seeds
1 lb (450 g) sushi-grade tuna
  fillet, cleaned and cubed
1 tsp (5 mL) peeled and
  minced fresh ginger
1½ Tbsp (23 mL) soy sauce
2 tsp (10 mL) fresh lime
  juice
1 small jalapeño chili, finely
  minced
1½ Tbsp (23 mL) toasted
  sesame oil
1 Tbsp (15 mL) finely
  chopped chives

Nouveau Niçoise Salad

When it comes to making niçoise salad, the art is in the presentation. Assemble this salad in any way you find appealing: mix the olives, tomatoes, green beans, potatoes, red onion, and caper berries and layer the tuna and egg on top; arrange the ingredients in rows; or plate the components in an abstract fashion on a large platter and have people assemble a salad for themselves.

Place the Dijon mustard, honey, vinegar, and tarragon in a small bowl and whisk to combine. Add 2 Tbsp (30 mL) of the olive oil in a slow, steady stream while whisking vigorously. The mixture should thicken and emulsify. Set aside the vinaigrette until you are ready to dress the salad.

Add the green beans to a medium-sized pot of boiling water. Cook 2 to 3 minutes—they should still be crunchy—and then place them in an ice-water bath (a large bowl filled with cold water and ice cubes). This will stop them cooking and keep them crunchy and green.

Place the eggs in the pot of boiling water. Cook at a rolling boil for 7 minutes, then remove eggs from the water and place in the ice bath briefly to stop the cooking. Leave in shells until ready to assemble salad.

Preparing the potatoes ahead of time makes for a much faster process. They can be boiled in advance in a pot of water with just a pinch of sea salt and kept in the fridge for up to 24 hours. To reheat, just drop them into the boiling bean/egg water for 30 seconds and then remove.

Preheat a large skillet over medium-high heat. Rub the tuna with the remaining 2 Tbsp (30 mL) of olive oil and season with a pinch of sea salt and pepper. Sear the tuna for approximately 2 minutes per side. Remove from the pan and slice thinly; the inside should still be a bit pink.

Peel the eggs and slice them in half length-wise. It's normal for the yolks to still be a bit soft or jammy.

Assemble the ingredients as you wish and either drizzle the salad with the vinaigrette or serve it on the side.

Serves 4

For the Vinaigrette
½ tsp (2.5 mL) Dijon mustard
1 tsp (5 mL) honey
1½ Tbsp (23 mL) white wine vinegar
1 Tbsp (15 mL) finely chopped fresh tarragon
4 Tbsp (60 mL) extra virgin olive oil

¼ lb (115 g) green beans, stems trimmed
4 large eggs
½ lb (225 g) new red potatoes, scrubbed, halved, and boiled until cooked
1 lb (450 g) fresh sushi-grade tuna
Sea salt and freshly ground black pepper
½ cup (125 mL) niçoise olives, pitting optional
1 cup (250 mL) cherry tomatoes, halved
½ medium red onion, peeled and thinly sliced
8 caper berries with stems

Sesame-Crusted Tuna with Wasabi Mashed Potatoes

If wasabi is not your cup of tea, this dish works well with buttermilk mashed potatoes or even a scented basmati rice.

In a large pot, cover the potatoes with water and bring to a boil. Cook until tender, 15 to 20 minutes. Drain the potatoes. In a small saucepan warm the half-and-half. Add the melted butter and wasabi and mix until combined. Add the wasabi mixture to the potatoes. Mash until smooth.

Season the tuna with the sea salt and black pepper. Place the sesame seeds in a shallow bowl or on a plate and coat the tuna, gently patting down on all sides to encourage the sesame seeds to stick. Over medium-high heat, add the grapeseed oil to a skillet. Cook the tuna for 1 minute on each side. Do not overcook.

To serve, cut the tuna steak into ½-inch-thick (1 cm) slices and plate with mash.

Serves 2

2 large russet potatoes, scrubbed, peeled, and cubed

⅓ cup (80 mL) half-and-half

¼ cup (60 mL) butter, melted

2 tsp (10 mL) wasabi paste

1 Pacific bluefin tuna steak, centre-cut, about 7 oz (200 g), 1½ inch (4 cm) thick

Sea salt and freshly cracked black pepper

2 Tbsp (30 mL) black sesame seeds (can use white or mixed)

2 tsp (10 mL) grapeseed oil

HALIBUT

Have you ever seen a halibut in the wild? They are *huge* and, let's be honest, fairly funny-looking. Most of us only experience these gentle giants as five-ounce fillet or steak portions, but the reality is that they are some of the biggest fish in our waters—and some of the most delicious, in our opinion. Halibut has a dense, thick meat that goes as well with heavy sauces such as our homemade tartar sauce as it does with light, citrus-y butter, making it one of the most versatile fish. We've included it in our chowders and pies as well—we love the richness halibut brings to any mixed seafood dish.

The Ocean Wise seafood program considers the Pacific halibut industry to be a model of sustainable fishing, so enjoy our local halibut knowing that you're having a low impact on halibut populations. Both common fishing methods—bottom long-line or hand-line—have extremely low levels of bycatch and cause minimal damage to the ocean floor.

Pacific Seafood Chowder

The base of this soup is a classic chowder stock, to which you can add any ingredients you wish. Try a smoked fish for intense flavour, and vary the vegetables according to what's in season and what you prefer.

Chop the halibut, salmon, prawns, and scallops into 1-inch (2.5 cm) pieces.

Heat the oil in a large saucepan over medium heat. Add the onion and celery, and cook until the onion is soft, about 8 to 10 minutes. Stir in the flour and cook another 2 minutes. While whisking constantly, slowly add the stock and simmer another 3 to 4 minutes. Add the potatoes and boil for 10 to 15 minutes or until the potatoes are cooked through.

Add the peas, cream, thyme leaves, paprika, and cayenne pepper. Stir until well combined.

Add the seafood and simmer for 10 minutes until it is cooked through. Season with salt and pepper to taste. Serve hot, garnished with thyme sprigs.

Serves 4 to 6

¼ lb (115 g) halibut
¼ lb (115 g) salmon
¼ lb (115 g) prawns
¼ lb (115 g) scallops
1 Tbsp (15 mL) vegetable oil
1 large onion, diced
½ cup diced celery
1 Tbsp (15 mL) flour
4 cups (1 L) vegetable or fish stock
½ lb (225 g) new potatoes, halved
1 cup (250 mL) fresh or frozen peas
1 cup (250 mL) cream
1 Tbsp (15 mL) fresh thyme leaves, plus sprigs for garnish
Pinch of paprika
Pinch of cayenne pepper
Sea salt and freshly cracked black pepper to taste

Mojito-Glazed Grilled Halibut

This recipe works on the grill as well as in the oven: simply cook the fillets at a medium-high temperature with the grill or BBQ lid closed for 3 minutes per side. Then flip the fish to serving-side up and cover the top of each fillet with half of the butter mixture. Let cook for another 2 to 3 minutes, then cover with the remainder of the butter mixture. Cook until the halibut is firm and flaky and the glaze is golden and sticky. Let sit 3 to 4 minutes before serving.

Place the butter, brown sugar, lime zest, lime juice, mint leaves, shallot, and garlic in a bowl. Mix to combine well and set aside.

Preheat the oven to 400°F (200°C).

Lightly season the halibut with the sea salt and black pepper, then place in a single layer in a baking dish. Cover the top of each piece of fish evenly with the butter mixture. Bake 10 to 12 minutes or until the halibut is firm and flaky. Turn the oven broiler to high and broil the top of the halibut for 1 to 2 minutes or until the glaze is bubbling and golden. Remove halibut from the oven and let sit for 3 to 4 minutes before serving.

Serves 4

¼ cup (60 mL) unsalted butter, softened
¼ cup (60 mL) brown sugar
2 Tbsp (30 mL) lime zest
2 Tbsp (30 mL) lime juice
2 Tbsp (30 mL) finely chopped fresh mint leaves
1 shallot, minced
1 garlic clove, minced
4 × 6 oz (170 g) halibut fillets
Pinch of sea salt
Pinch of freshly cracked black pepper

Potato-Wrapped Halibut

This recipe is a variation on one Danielle learned years ago while working at Dish Cooking Studio in Toronto; it's a fun, fancy version of fish and chips. It pairs well with the Tartar Sauce (page 148) or the Rémoulade (page 149), as well as any of the flavoured aiolis (page 149).

Preheat oven to 400°F (200°C).

Line a baking sheet with parchment paper. Using a mandolin, slice the potatoes very thinly lengthwise. Arrange them in 4 lines, overlapping the slices widthwise, like scales. Place in the oven for 6 to 7 minutes or until the potatoes are pliable.

Remove the baking sheet from the oven and place one halibut fillet on each line of potatoes. Season with salt and pepper, and then wrap the potato "scales" around the halibut pieces.

Raise the oven heat to 450°F (230°C).

In a large frying pan, heat the olive oil over medium-high heat and sauté the fillets on all sides until they are a light golden brown. Remove the fillets from the skillet and place them back on the parchment-lined baking sheet. Bake for 5 to 7 minutes or until the fish is mostly firm to the touch. Let fillets rest 1 to 2 minutes. Serve with Tartar Sauce.

Serves 4

3 to 4 Yukon Gold potatoes, peeled
4 × 5 oz (140 g) halibut fillets, skin removed
Salt and pepper to taste
2 Tbsp (30 mL) olive oil
1 cup (250 mL) Tartar Sauce (page 148)

West Coast Fish Pie

This recipe works well with any sort of fish you wish to incorporate. Feel free to substitute crab and shrimp for the meaty fishes here, or add scallops for an even richer flavour.

Preheat oven to 375°F (190°C).

Defrost 2 sheets of puff pastry to room temperature.

Heat a high-sided skillet. Once it's hot, add the olive oil and fish and sear gently for 1 to 2 minutes. Then place the fish on a plate and remove the pan from the heat.

Add ¼ cup (60 mL) of butter and the flour to the skillet and cook over medium heat until the butter is melted and the mixture begins to turn slightly brown. Slowly add the milk while whisking constantly. Mix in the Dijon mustard and nutmeg. Return the mixture to medium heat and cook until slightly thickened, stirring frequently. Once thickened, add the fish and peas. Cook another 2 to 3 minutes, mixing the ingredients to combine well. Remove from heat and let cool slightly. Stir in the chopped eggs and season lightly with a pinch of salt and pepper.

Pour the fish mixture into a 12-cup (3 L) casserole dish.

Place one sheet of puff pastry on top of the other and roll out together to ¼" thickness. Place on top of casserole dish and crimp to finish the edge. Beat egg yolk with 1 Tbsp milk and brush the top of the pastry. Bake on the centre rack of the oven for approximately 30 minutes or until the potato topping is golden and the filling is bubbly around the edges. Remove from oven and let rest at least 5 minutes. Serve warm.

Serves 6 to 8

1 package frozen puff pastry

¼ cup (125 mL) unsalted butter

2 Tbsp (30 mL) olive oil

1 lb (450 g) sablefish, cut into 1-inch (2.5 cm) cubes

1 lb (450 g) salmon, cut into 1-inch (2.5 cm) cubes

1 lb (450 g) halibut, cut into 1-inch (2.5 cm) cubes

3 Tbsp (45 mL) flour

2 cups (500 mL) milk

2 Tbsp (30 mL) Dijon mustard

1 tsp (5 mL) freshly grated nutmeg

1 cup (250 mL) fresh or frozen peas

4 large hard-boiled eggs, peeled and chopped into large chunks

1 cup (250 mL) grated cheddar cheese

2 pinches of sea salt

2 pinches of freshly cracked black pepper

Pan-Seared Halibut Cheeks with Citrus Brown Butter Sauce

This recipe and method also works with halibut steaks and fillets—don't forget to increase the cooking time to ensure the fish is cooked through.

Season the halibut cheeks lightly with salt and pepper, and let them come to room temperature.

In a medium-sized frying pan over medium heat, place the butter, citrus juices, citrus zests, and garlic. Heat until the butter is melted, stirring to combine well. Place the cheeks in the pan, spooning the butter sauce over them so they become well coated. Cook 2 to 3 minutes per side, constantly basting with the citrus butter. Serve warm with the butter sauce drizzled over top.

Serves 4

8 halibut cheeks
Sea salt and freshly cracked
   black pepper to taste
3 Tbsp (45 mL) butter
1 Tbsp (15 mL) lemon juice
1 Tbsp (15 mL) orange juice
½ tsp (2.5 mL) freshly grated
   lemon zest
½ tsp (2.5 mL) grated
   orange zest
¼ tsp (1 mL) grated
   lime zest
1 small garlic clove, minced

SABLEFISH

Never heard of sablefish? How about black cod? This gorgeous, succulent, and oh-so-delicious species seems to go by a different name depending which side of the Canada/US border you're cooking on. But the results are the same, and dishes prepared with this rich white meat promise to be both hearty and satisfying. With its dense texture, sablefish holds up well to heavy glazes and is also a welcome addition to seafood soups and pastas, as it tends to have a light oil that deepens the flavour of any dish it's added to. If sablefish happens to be fresh and available at your local market, it can easily be used in place of halibut for any of the recipes in this book.

Sablefish are part of the family known as "groundfish," and bycatch can be a concern with them. Environmental damage caused by bottom trawling is being mitigated by regulations defining fishing grounds, but we tend to seek out longline-caught sablefish, which offers a bit more reassurance that every precaution possible has been taken in terms of responsible fishing.

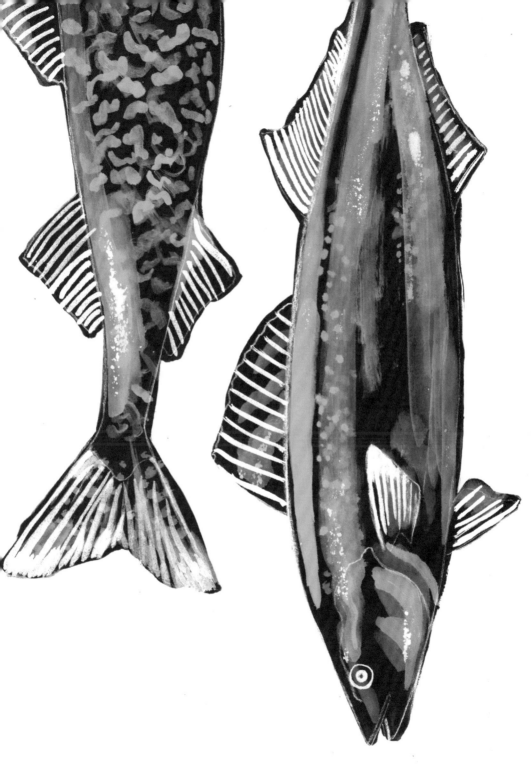

Miso Ginger Glazed Sablefish

Sablefish is one of the most versatile fish to cook with. Its hearty, meaty texture and subtle flavour make it perfect for pairing with several different glazes. Instead of ginger, try using sriracha or sambal oelek for a hit of spiciness.

Combine the miso, mirin, rice vinegar, and ginger in a bowl and set aside.

Preheat the oven to 400°F (200°C).

Lightly season the sablefish fillets with salt and place them on a foil-lined baking sheet. Drizzle the miso mixture over the fish and place the baking sheet on the middle rack of the oven. Bake for 5 minutes, then baste or brush the fish with the mixture. Repeat 2 to 3 times. Bake 10 to 15 minutes total or until the fish is slightly firm to the touch.

Serves 4

1 Tbsp (15 mL) white miso
1 Tbsp (15 mL) mirin
2 tsp (10 mL) rice vinegar
1 Tbsp (15 mL) freshly
   grated ginger
4 × 6 oz (170 g) sablefish
   fillets, skin on
Pinch of sea salt

Tomato Turmeric Grilled Sablefish

This marinade works well with sablefish, halibut, or any other hearty white fish that is in season.

Preheat the grill to medium heat.

In a blender, combine all ingredients except for the sablefish and mix on high for 1 minute. Pour the resulting marinade into a shallow dish and lay the sablefish on top. Cover the fish with the marinade and let it sit for 10 minutes.

Grill the fish for 5 to 6 minutes. Flip, then baste with the marinade. Cook another 5 minutes. Flip and baste once more. Cook another 2 minutes. Remove from heat and serve.

Serves 4

5 sweet vine-ripened cherry tomatoes

2-inch (5 cm) piece of turmeric, grated

¼ cup (60 mL) olive oil

2 tsp (10 mL) balsamic vinegar

1 tsp (5 mL) smoked paprika

1 Tbsp (15 mL) chopped fresh rosemary

1 Tbsp (15 mL) fresh thyme, stems removed

1 Tbsp (15 mL) chopped fresh basil

½ tsp (2.5 mL) sea salt

¼ tsp (1 mL) freshly cracked black pepper

1 side of sablefish, approx. 1 lb (450 g)

COD

To my mind, cod is the real chicken of the sea: it can be used in so many dishes, and it goes well with whatever sauce or accompaniment is added to it. We love it in soups and tacos, or as the preferred fish in fish and chips. While it doesn't have the meatiness of halibut or sablefish, cod's light and delicate texture makes it a favourite of children and a welcome addition to any chowder or pie.

The word cod can raise concern in those who care about fish populations. But while the Atlantic cod industry has reached a critical state, the Pacific cod industry here on the West Coast is being monitored closely to ensure that strict regulations are being followed. Cod and lingcod are both part of the groundfish family and as such are protected in many locations; fishing only occurs in areas that can withstand it, to ensure that minimal environmental impact occurs.

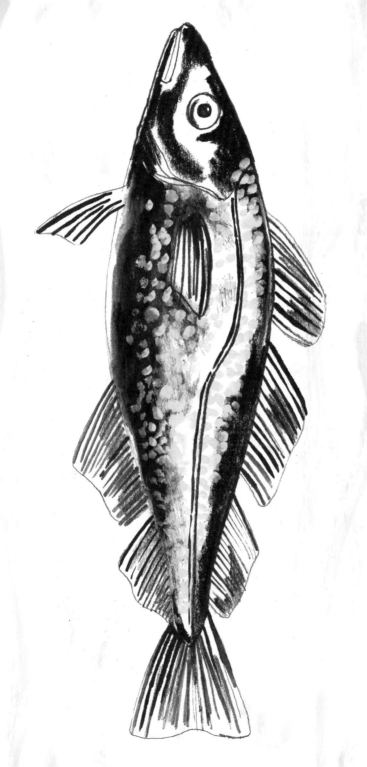

Blackened Cod Tacos with Chipotle Peach Salsa and Slaw

Halibut, sablefish, or snapper also works well in these tacos—the key is to use a nice, fresh white fish that doesn't have too strong a flavour profile.

In a large bowl, combine the smoked paprika, chili powder, oregano, thyme, onion powder, garlic powder, cumin, sea salt, and freshly cracked black pepper. Add the fish and coat well with the spice mix.

Heat the oil over medium high heat. Add the fish and cook 4 minutes per side.

For the salsa, combine the peaches, red bell pepper, tomatoes, jalapeño, chipotle pepper, cilantro, lime juice, honey, and sea salt. Mix well.

For the slaw, combine the cabbage, lime juice, and sea salt. Toss well to combine.

To serve, place some slaw, fish, and salsa in each tortilla.

Serves 4

1 tsp (5 mL) smoked paprika
1 tsp (5 mL) chili powder
1 tsp (5 mL) dried oregano
1 tsp (5 mL) dried thyme
1 tsp (5 mL) dried onion powder
1 tsp (5 mL) garlic powder
1 tsp (5 mL) cumin
1 tsp (5 mL) sea salt
¼ tsp (1 mL) black pepper
1 lb (450 g) rock cod
1 Tbsp (15 mL) olive oil

For the Salsa

2 ripe peaches, pitted and diced
¼ cup (60 mL) red bell pepper, diced
¼ cup (60 mL) diced cherry tomatoes
1 small jalapeño, minced
1 chipotle pepper, diced
2 Tbsp (30 mL) chopped cilantro
3 Tbsp (45 mL) lime juice
2 Tbsp (30 mL) honey
½ tsp (2.5 mL) sea salt

For the Slaw

2 cups (500 mL) thinly sliced
  cabbage
3 Tbsp (45 mL) lime juice
¼ tsp (1 mL) sea salt

8 small tortillas, warmed

Cod *en Papillote* with Herb Butter

Sablefish or halibut will work equally well here, but both are much richer and denser than the delicate cod. Be sure to adjust the cooking time to the density of the fish: for sablefish and halibut, add 5 to 7 minutes to the cooking time and let rest a minute longer afterward.

The instructions below call for one large piece of fish, but you can also divide the fish, herbed butter, and tomato olive mixture into four servings and create individual packages for a more formal serving presentation.

Place the butter in a bowl and add the ½ cup (125 mL) chopped fresh herbs. Using a spatula, mix together until well combined. Cover with plastic wrap and place in the fridge to harden, about two hours.

Preheat the oven to 375°F (190°C). In a bowl, combine the cherry tomatoes, Kalamata olives, garlic, thyme leaves, olive oil, lemon zest, and sea salt. Place a large piece of parchment paper on a baking sheet. Lay the cod on the top half of the parchment paper. Spread the herbed butter across the fish and top with the tomato/olive mixture.

Fold the lower half of the parchment paper over the fish. Then starting at one corner and working your way around, fold the two edges of the parchment paper together, pleating all around the fish to form a fully enveloped package. Bake on the baking sheet for 25 to 30 minutes. Remove from the oven and let the fish rest for 5 minutes before serving.

Serves 4

½ cup (125 mL) butter, room temperature

½ cup (125 mL) chopped fresh herbs, such as thyme, parsley, rosemary, or chives

½ cup (125 mL) halved cherry tomatoes

¼ cup (60 mL) pitted and halved Kalamata olives

1 garlic clove, finely chopped or grated

1 tsp (5 mL) thyme leaves

1 Tbsp (15 mL) olive oil

1 lemon, zested and sliced

½ tsp (2.5 mL) sea salt

1 lb (450 g) cod

English-Style Beer-Battered Lingcod

If you're new to deep-frying, don't be daunted: it's quite easy. The trick is to keep an eye on the temperature of the oil—if it gets too hot, the outside of the fish will cook too quickly and the inside won't get the heat it needs. If the oil isn't hot enough, the batter will absorb too much oil and won't become the light, crispy texture you're looking for. A good candy/deep-fry thermometer secured to the side of your saucepan will make monitoring the oil temperature easy.

In a large mixing bowl, combine the flour, cornstarch, baking powder, paprika, and white pepper; then remove ½ cup (125 mL) of these dry ingredients and set aside. While whisking, slowly add the beer to the main bowl and mix until you have a smooth batter. Let rest for at least 30 minutes.

Using a candy/deep-fry thermometer to monitor the temperature, heat the oil in a deep saucepan to 350°F (180°C). Drop a small amount of batter into the oil—it should sizzle and crisp up quickly. Lay the strips of cod on a paper towel to dry and pat away any excess moisture. Toss the fish in the set-aside dry-ingredient mixture. Then working piece by piece, dip each strip into the batter and place it carefully in the heated oil. Deep-fry for 6 to 8 minutes or until the fish is crispy and golden. Using a large slotted spoon, lift out each piece, drain on a paper towel, and sprinkle with sea salt.

Serves 2

1½ cups (375 mL)
  all-purpose flour
½ cup (125 mL) cornstarch
1 Tbsp (15 mL) baking
  powder
1 tsp (5 mL) paprika
  (optional)
1 tsp (5 mL) white pepper
12 oz (355 mL) bottle of
  your favourite lager
  or pale ale
4 cups (1 L) safflower
  or canola oil
1 lb (450 g) fillet lingcod,
  cut into about 6 × 2-inch-
  wide (5 cm) strips
Pinch of sea salt

ROCKFISH + SMELT

We couldn't write a West Coast seafood cookbook without including two more fish. Rockfish are extremely prevalent in these waters and are often caught in conjunction with cod and halibut, while smelt is a fish with a long history of use with the local peoples.

Rockfish—a general name for a wide range of bottom-dwelling fish—are usually further distinguished by colour: red rockfish, blue rockfish, tiger-striped rockfish, etc. BC's local snapper falls into this category as well. The flesh of rockfish is light in colour and extremely delicate in taste. It can easily replace cod in tacos, is lovely battered in place of lingcod, and is a wonderful addition to soups and curries. This is a great fish to grill whole, as in the Fire-Roasted Whole Pacific Salmon on page 34, but we also love it with Asian flavours—ginger, sesame oil, cilantro, or Thai chilies instead of lemon and fresh herbs. The skin will be nice and crispy and the flesh will easily fall away from the bone with the aid of a fork.

BC smelt are anadromous fish, which means they leave salt water to breed in fresh water. You may know them by their Indigenous name, oolichan, or as candlefish—aptly named, as their flesh is extremely oily and they can be burned much like candles when dried. These beautiful fish are perfect for grilling whole, and if you love herring kippers for breakfast, you're going to want to try these in their place.

Curried Rockfish Hot Pot

The rockfish in this recipe is representative of any light, white fish that is in season: snapper, rock cod, and lingcod are also good options. Alternatively, you can use prawns, allowing 4 to 5 per person. There are many varieties of Thai curries (red, green, yellow, etc.). Feel free to experiment to find out which you think goes best with the fish—we prefer red, but if you like it hot, try the green.

In an 8 to 10 inch (20 to 25 cm) pot, heat the oil to medium high and add the onion. Cook for 5 minutes until softened and translucent. Stir in the ginger, garlic, and chili, and cook an additional 2 to 3 minutes. Add the curry paste, brown sugar, and rice vinegar, stirring until the sugar begins to melt. Add the tomatoes, coconut milk, and fish sauce and reduce heat to a simmer.

Place the fish chunks in the pot and cover it with a lid. Let simmer for 5 minutes. Remove the lid and add the lime juice and half of the cilantro. Continue to simmer an additional 4 to 5 minutes; the fish is cooked when it is light and flaky throughout. Serve alongside rice and garnish with a lime wedge and the remaining cilantro.

Serves 4

1 Tbsp (15 mL) vegetable oil
1 medium onion, finely chopped
3-inch (7.5 cm) length of fresh ginger, finely grated
4 garlic cloves, minced
1 small red chili, thinly sliced (optional)
2 Tbsp (30 mL) Thai-style red curry paste
1 Tbsp (15 mL) brown sugar
1 Tbsp (15 mL) rice vinegar
18 oz (540 mL) can of diced tomatoes
13 oz (400 mL) can of coconut milk
1 tsp (5 mL) fish sauce
1 lb (450 g) of skinless rockfish fillet, cut into 1-inch-long (2.5 cm) chunks
Juice of 1 lime, freshly squeezed
1 small bunch of cilantro, coarsely chopped
1 lime, quartered for serving

Grilled Whole Smelt
with Sweet Chili Lemon Sauce

Smelt under 6 inches long can be grilled whole, head and insides intact. If you're working with slightly bigger fish or if cooking whole fish makes you uneasy, have your fishmonger clean them for you. For cleaned fish, reduce the cooking time by 1 or 2 minutes per side.

Cut the lemons in half and set aside.

In a large baking dish, add the olive oil, minced garlic, red pepper flakes, lemon zest, and sea salt, stirring to combine. Place the smelt in the marinade and let stand for 30 to 60 minutes.

Heat a charcoal or gas grill to medium high. Place the smelt directly on the grill. Add the lemons, cut side down, to the grill. Cook the smelt for 4 to 5 minutes per side or until deep golden brown. Remove the smelt and the lemons from the grill.

Divide the fish between 4 plates and squeeze the grilled lemons over top. Serve with Sweet Chili Lemon Sauce.

Serves 4

2 lemons
¼ cup (60 mL) olive oil
1 clove of garlic, minced
2 tsp (10 mL) red pepper flakes
1 tsp (5 mL) freshly grated lemon zest
1 tsp (5 mL) sea salt
1 lb (450 g) fresh smelt, heads on
1 cup (250 mL) Sweet Chili Lemon Sauce (page 151)

SHRIMP
and
PRAWNS
and
CRAB,
Oh My!

One of the ocean's greatest gifts is glorious, beautiful shellfish. The hard part is choosing which is your favourite. Whether it's with your eggs at breakfast on a seafood Benedict, as crab cakes with salad for a light lunch, or hot off the grill with homemade aioli for dinner, the versatile Dungeness crab from our local waters is a perfect treat any time of day. Dungeness crabs are best eaten fresh from the sea—toss them straight from the ocean into a pot of boiling sea water and serve them up with ice-cold beer, lemon wedges, and your sauce of choice (Aurelia and I like a simple aioli and some Louisiana hot sauce) for the ultimate in perfection and simplicity. Of course, if you don't have direct access to crab traps, a good fishmonger will have them live and will be able to flash-clean them for you so they're ready for your pot as soon as you can get them there. And if cracking through a crab's hefty shell isn't your idea of fun, your local merchant should have fresh, ready-to-use crabmeat.

But what of the enormous variety of shrimp available on the West Coast? Tiny shrimp for dumplings and in place of crab in seafood Benedict; medium-sized shrimp for cioppino, fritters, and sweet and sour shrimp balls; and jumbo shrimp for shrimp rolls and ceviche—the possibilities for these gloriously succulent crustaceans seem limitless. We've assigned prawns to some of our recipes, but larger shrimp can easily be used in their place.

Of course, in the psyche of West Coast cooks, no one ranks higher among crustaceans than spot prawns. Their season is short—just four to six weeks out of every year—and thus when we can get them, we eat as many as possible. I love them as the stars of a simple peel 'n' eat platter or the Tofino Beach Party Boil. They can replace shrimp in any of the recipes included here, and they make a good addition to many a pasta dish. They're available frozen throughout the year, but as with all seafood, they can't be beat when they're fresh as can be.

Sustainability and environmental protection are important considerations when choosing your shellfish. Aim for trap-caught crab, shrimp, and prawns as opposed to bottom-trawled ones: although efforts are made to reduce the impact to the ocean floor when trawling, traps are still less invasive and produce less bycatch than netting does. The West Coast of Canada produces only about 1 percent of all shrimp pulled in North America, and spot prawns, with their short season, are very well managed here, so go ahead and enjoy your well-fished shellfish in good conscience.

Shrimp & Prawns
✳ ✳ ✳

Classic Peel 'n' Eat Prawns **82**

Spot Prawn and Sweet Corn Fritters **84**

The Perfect Shrimp Bisque **85**

Coconut Prawns with Sriracha Aioli **86**

Sweet and Sour Shrimp Balls **88**

Shrimp Dumplings with Spicy Sesame Dipping Sauce **90**

West Coast Shrimp Roll **92**

Crab

✳ ✳ ✳

SHRIMP + PRAWNS

We love prawns so much here in BC that every May, there's a festival in Vancouver to mark the beginning of spot prawn season. Spot prawns are the most beautiful and flavourful of our local prawns and, as their season is only four to six weeks long, every bite you get to enjoy is indeed worthy of celebration. Of course, this is only one of many species available locally; your fishmonger should have some fresh, live prawns on hand when they're in season. If not, they will often carry a "frozen at sea" selection, which means the crustaceans were plunged into a severe deep freeze right after being caught, ensuring they stay fresh and that their texture is as close to live as possible.

If cleaning shrimp or prawns seems like a hassle, you can ask your fishmonger to de-head and devein them, but it's not that hard. A simple twist will remove the head. A pair of kitchen snips along the back of the shell plus a wipe with a knife down the dark "vein" underneath, and you're good to go. A bonus of doing it yourself is that the shells and heads make the perfect base for a delicious fish stock.

Classic Peel 'n' Eat Prawns

This recipe includes a seafood seasoning made from scratch, but if you happen to have a product like Old Bay on hand, that will work too. The seasoning here is delicious with boiled prawns, shrimp, crab, or lobster. If you prefer even more flavour, leave the prawn heads on during boiling.

Place the dry spices in a bowl and mix to combine. Remove 1 Tbsp (15 mL) of the spice mixture and set aside.

Fill an extra-large pot two-thirds of the way up with water. Add the larger portion of the spice mix, along with the lager, garlic, bay leaves, and cloves. Bring to a rolling boil and keep there at least 5 minutes.

Fill a colander with ice and place it inside a larger bowl (for draining the water away). Have more ice on hand and ready. Place the prawns in the boiling water and stand by—they cook quickly and you don't want to overcook them. Prawns are ready to be removed from the water when they float and are pink all over.

Remove cooked prawns from the water with a slotted spoon and immediately chill on ice in the fridge. When you're ready to serve them, dust the prawns with the re-served 1 Tbsp (15 mL) of spice mixture. Serve chilled with Classic Cocktail Sauce.

Serves 6 to 8

2 Tbsp (30 mL) celery seeds
2 Tbsp (30 mL) sea salt
4 tsp (20 mL) freshly ground black pepper
4 tsp (20 mL) red pepper flakes
4 tsp (20 mL) smoked paprika
2 tsp (10 mL) dry English mustard
1 tsp (5 mL) nutmeg
1 tsp (5 mL) ground cinnamon
11 oz (330 mL) bottle of your favourite lager or ale
4 cloves of garlic
3 bay leaves
8 whole cloves
2 to 3 lbs (1 to 1.5 kg) prawns (26 to 30 per pound), de-headed, shells split, and deveined
Classic Cocktail Sauce (page 148)

Spot Prawn and Sweet Corn Fritters

We've used spot prawns here because they are particularly juicy and delectable, but any good-sized prawns or shrimp will work. If you don't have access to chickpea flour, a good-quality brown rice flour will work, or white flour if that's all you have; they will just result in a lighter batter.

Fill a large, high-walled skillet or cast-iron Dutch oven with 3 to 4 inches (8 to 10 cm) of vegetable oil. Using a candy/deep-fry thermometer to monitor, heat the oil to 370°F (190°C).

In a large bowl, place the chickpea flour, spot prawns, onion, corn, cilantro, red pepper flakes, baking powder, and sea salt. Mix well to combine.

While mixing vigorously with a wooden spoon, slowly add the water until the batter has the thick consistency of Greek yogurt and is slightly bubbly throughout.

Using two spoons and working in small batches, carefully place heaping tablespoons of batter in the hot oil. Deep-fry until the fritters turn a deep golden brown, about 2 to 3 minutes per side. Drain on paper towels, then serve immediately with Sweet Chili Dipping Sauce.

Makes 24 fritters

Vegetable oil for deep-frying
2 cups (500 mL) chickpea flour
½ lb (225 g) raw, de-headed, peeled, and deveined spot prawns, roughly chopped
½ medium yellow onion, finely diced
½ cup (125 mL) fresh or defrosted frozen corn kernels
½ cup (125 mL) chopped cilantro leaves
1 Tbsp (15 mL) red pepper flakes
½ tsp (2.5 mL) baking powder
½ tsp (2.5 mL) sea salt
Up to 1 cup (250 mL) lukewarm water
Sweet Chili Dipping Sauce (page 151)

The Perfect Shrimp Bisque

This recipe comes from Victoria chef Maggie Aro and is quite simply the best we've ever had! If you want the bisque to be thick and creamy, you can use an egg yolk to thicken it. Before adding the shrimp meat whisk an egg yolk in a small bowl, add ½ cup (125 mL) of hot soup, then pour the mixture into the pot. Whisk until well blended, then add the shrimp meat. Try this recipe with prawns, crab, lobster, or langoustines—it works perfectly with any tasty crustacean.

Cook the shrimp with shells on in boiling water until just done: 2 to 4 minutes, depending on size. Remove the shrimp from the pot and reserve 4 cups (1 L) of cooking liquid for soup base. Let the shrimp cool. Peel, and reserve the shells for the soup base and the meat for the finish.

To make the soup base, melt 2 Tbsp (30 mL) butter in a pot over medium heat. Combine the chopped shallots and chopped garlic cloves and add a ½ cup (125 mL) of the mixture to the butter; let cook for 3 minutes. Add the reserved shells and tomato paste. Stir well and let cook for about a minute. Add the carrot, celery, and wine, and cook to let the wine reduce by half, about 5 minutes. Add the reserved cooking liquid, parsley, thyme, red pepper flakes, and bay leaf. Simmer for 30 minutes. Strain into a bowl. Discard the solids. You should have 3 to 4 cups (750 mL to 1 L) of liquid.

In a stock pot, melt 2 Tbsp (30 mL) of butter. Add remaining ¼ cup (60 mL) of garlic and shallots and cook about 2 minutes. Stir in the flour and cook about 1 minute. Slowly whisk in 3 cups (750 mL) of the strained shrimp stock, making sure it's well blended. Whisk in the milk and whipping cream. Heat until hot, but do not let it boil rapidly. Season to taste with sea salt and pepper. Stir in the shrimp meat and serve immediately. If the bisque is too thick, adjust with the reserved stock.

Serves 6

1 lb (450 g) shrimp with shells, heads, and tails on

8 cups (2 L) water

¼ cup (60 mL) butter, divided

¾ cup (185 mL) finely chopped shallots

2 cloves of garlic, crushed and chopped

3 Tbsp (45 mL) tomato paste

1 carrot, peeled and roughly chopped

1 celery rib, chopped

2 cups (500 mL) dry white wine

1 parsley stem

1 sprig of thyme

Pinch of red pepper flakes

1 bay leaf

2 Tbsp (30 mL) flour

2 cups (500 mL) milk

¾ cup (185 mL) whipping cream

Pinch of sea salt, to taste

Pinch of white pepper, to taste

Coconut Prawns with Sriracha Aioli

These can easily serve as party hors d'oeuvres if you use slightly smaller prawns and double the recipe.

In a bowl, combine the panko and shredded coconut. Crack the eggs into another bowl, and beat. In a third bowl, place the flour, sea salt, and black pepper.

One at a time, dredge the prawns in the flour mixture, then the egg, then the panko/coconut mixture. Set aside on a plate until all the prawns have been coated.

In a large high-walled skillet, heat the oil to 370°F (190°C) using a deep-fry/candy thermometer to monitor. In batches so as not to overcrowd, cook the prawns 2 minutes per side, until golden brown. Then using a slotted spoon, remove the prawns and lay them on a tray lined with paper towels.

Serve with Sriracha Aioli.

Serves 4

1 cup (250 mL) panko bread crumbs
1 cup (250 mL) unsweetened shredded coconut
2 large eggs
½ cup (125 mL) flour
¼ tsp (1 mL) sea salt
¼ tsp (1 mL) freshly cracked black pepper
1 lb (450 g) raw prawns, deheaded, peeled, deveined, and tail on
2 cups (500 mL) coconut oil (or preferred frying oil)
½ cup (125 mL) Sriracha Aioli (page 149)

Sweet and Sour Shrimp Balls

These shrimp "meatballs" are an easy party appetizer that can be made ahead of time, refrigerated, and warmed in the oven when ready to serve. Feel free to play with the flavour profile and swap the sriracha for a little curry paste and finely chopped lemongrass for more of a Thai vibe or teriyaki sauce for a Japanese one. If you can't find tapioca flour or don't happen to have some on hand, you can make do with cornstarch in a pinch.

In a food processor, pulse the shrimp and water chestnuts until finely chopped.

In a bowl, combine the ground pork, rice vinegar, tapioca flour, ginger, chives, sriracha, and sea salt. Add the shrimp and water chestnut mixture to the pork mixture and mix well.

In a bowl, beat the egg whites until thick and frothy. Add to the shrimp/pork mixture and fold in until just combined.

Heat the oil in a wok or high-sided frying pan over medium-high heat. Using either your hands or 2 tablespoons, form the shrimp/pork mixture into 24 × 1½ inch (4 cm) balls. Using a slotted spoon, lower the shrimp balls into the hot oil and deep-fry for approximately 2 minutes or until they pop up in the pan and are a crispy golden brown—be sure to "turn" them with a wooden spoon so that all sides cook. Drain on paper towels and serve warm with Sweet and Sour Sauce.

Makes 2 dozen balls

2 lb (900 g) shrimp, de-headed, peeled, deveined, and tails removed
8 oz (1 cup; 250 mL) can of water chestnuts, drained and rinsed
6 oz (170 g) ground pork
2 Tbsp (30 mL) rice vinegar
2 Tbsp (30 mL) tapioca flour
1 inch (2.5 cm) piece of ginger, finely grated
2 Tbsp (30 mL) finely chopped chives
1 tsp (5 mL) sriracha or other hot sauce
2 tsp (10 mL) sea salt
3 egg whites
3 cups (750 mL) vegetable oil for frying
Sweet and Sour Sauce (page 151)

Shrimp Dumplings with Spicy Sesame Dipping Sauce

This is our favourite recipe in the book! Don't be daunted by the handmade dough—it's just flour and water and a little elbow grease. Still, store-bought wonton wrappers will work just as well: you'll need about 36 wrappers.

Combine the flour and warm water and form a dough. Knead the dough until smooth, about two minutes. Cover in plastic and let rest for 30 minutes.

Finely chop the shrimp. Place in a medium bowl and combine with the ginger, scallions, and Napa cabbage.

Prepare a lightly floured surface. Pinch off a 1-inch (2.5 cm) piece of dough and roll out into a circle ⅛-inch thick. Place 1 Tbsp (15 mL) of the shrimp mixture in the centre and fold the circle in half, pinching the two sides together to form a half-moon shape. Continue forming dumplings with remainder of dough. Place the dumplings on a lightly floured tea towel and place another towel on top so they don't dry out as you're making them.

In a large skillet, heat ¼ cup (60 mL) of water and 1 Tbsp (15 mL) of oil. Arrange the dumplings in a single layer and cover with a lid. Cook over medium heat until the water has evaporated and the dumplings are sizzling and golden on the bottom.

For the dipping sauce, combine the soy sauce, fish sauce, sesame oil, sriracha, coconut sugar, and scallion. Serve with the dumplings.

Makes 3 dozen dumplings

1 cup (250 mL) flour
½ cup (125 mL) warm water
¾ lb (340 g) raw shrimp, deheaded, peeled, deveined, and tails removed
2-inch (5 cm) piece of ginger, peeled and finely grated
3 scallions, finely chopped
1½ cup (375 mL) finely chopped Napa cabbage
¼ cup (60 mL) water
1 Tbsp (15 mL) olive oil
¼ cup (60 mL) soy sauce
2 Tbsp (30 mL) fish sauce
2 Tbsp (30 mL) sesame oil
1 Tbsp (15 mL) sriracha or sambal oelek
1 Tbsp (15 mL) coconut sugar or white sugar
1 scallion, finely chopped

West Coast Shrimp Roll

This recipe is a twist on the classic East Coast lobster roll. Here on the West Coast, we have some of the most delicious cold-water shrimp in the world, so why not try them in a roll? If spot prawns are in season, they're perfect as well. Flash-frozen shrimp will work here, but fresh is always better.

If you can't find top-split sandwich buns, any good kaiser-style buns will work.

In a large frying pan over high heat, place the olive oil, shrimp, celery, and paprika. Sauté 2 to 3 minutes or just until the shrimp turns a deep pink and the celery begins to soften. Remove from heat, set aside, and cool.

In a large bowl, place the cooled shrimp mixture. Add the aioli, green onion, lemon juice, sea salt, black pepper, and sriracha. Stir to combine well. Chill for 5 to 10 minutes while preparing buns.

Preheat the oven broiler to low. Brush the inside of each bun half with the melted butter and place the opened buns under the broiler for 1 to 2 minutes or just until the edges and inside of the buns start to crisp and turn golden. Remove from the oven and rub the inside of each bun with the freshly cut side of the garlic clove.

Fill each bun with a quarter of the chilled shrimp mixture. Garnish each plate with a lemon wedge and serve immediately.

Serves 4

- 1 Tbsp (15 mL) olive oil
- 2 lbs (900 g) shrimp, de-headed, peeled, deveined, tails removed, and cut into ½ inch (1 cm) pieces
- ¼ cup (60 mL) chopped celery
- ½ tsp (2.5 mL) smoked paprika
- ½ cup (125 mL) Aioli (page 149) or store-bought mayonnaise
- ¼ cup (60 mL) chopped green onion
- 1 Tbsp (15 mL) freshly squeezed lemon juice
- ½ tsp (2.5 mL) sea salt
- ½ tsp (2.5 mL) freshly cracked black pepper
- Dash sriracha or other hot sauce, to taste
- 4 top-split sandwich buns
- 2 Tbsp (30 mL) melted butter
- 1 clove of garlic, skin removed and sliced in half
- Lemon wedges for serving

CRAB

BC Dungeness crab are a local treasure. Slightly smaller than their king-sized cousins to the north, Dungeness are the perfect size for steaming, barbecuing, or adding to a "beach boil." Their meat is dense, flavourful, and perfect for all manner of dishes from eggs Benedict to crab cakes, making them one of the most coveted types of seafood in our kitchen. We love them barbecued with little more than a good jot of homemade aioli on the side. And Aurelia's cheesy, crabby Hasselback Potatoes are a dream for any seafood lover, and the perfect side for steak if you want to do a twist on surf 'n' turf.

If you're lucky enough to be able to throw your own traps in the water and pull up some crabs, be sure you keep only the mature males—females must be thrown back. Most good fishmongers will have live crabs in tanks when they're in season and will be happy to clean them for you, but so you can give it a try yourself, we've included easy, step-by-step instructions:

How to Clean a Crab

We'll admit it: cleaning crabs wasn't the simplest task when we were learning to cook seaside seafood, but once you get these 6 steps down, the process is quick and painless. We can't repeat enough how much easier it is to clean crabs underwater—it's a lot less messy when the ocean carries away the debris.

1. **Cook, then cool.** Be sure to let crabs cool completely so as not to scald your hands. This can be done in shallow sea waters. If you're cooking at home, place them in a large colander and run cold water over them for 5 minutes.
2. **Break off the apron.** At the bottom of the belly, there is a little tail-like piece. Use your thumb to snap it off.
3. **Remove the back shell.** This is best done underwater. Stick your thumb into the hole left by the apron and pull the back shell off—it will come away with lots of innards attached. Discard the shell and innards.
4. **Remove the gills and mouth.** Pull away the spongy, inedible gills on either side of the body and break away the spiny mouth pieces at the front of the crab.
5. **Rinse.** Rinse away all remaining innards, leaving just the cooked flesh and legs.
6. **Halve.** With a knife or using your hands, cut or break the crab in half—we like to serve one half per person.

Crab and Avocado Seafood Benedict

If you don't have the Smoked Salmon Terrine on hand, cream cheese can take its place. This is a classic eggs Benedict recipe with a seafood twist, and really, there are many variations that can be made using other recipes in this book: try topping cream cheese with the Beet-Cured Gravlax and avocado, or the Shrimp Roll filling and avocado. It's hard to go wrong with well-poached eggs and hollandaise sauce.

Turn the oven to the lowest baking temperature.

Using a toaster, toast the 4 bagel halves and spread equal portions of the Smoked Salmon Terrine on them. Top each with the crabmeat and avocado. Place on a baking sheet in the warmed oven.

Fill a medium-sized pot with 3 to 4 inches (7.5 to 10 cm) of water and add the vinegar. Bring the water to a low boil, then reduce the temperature to bring it to a simmer. Crack the eggs one at a time into a small bowl (to ensure the yolks do not break) and carefully slide each egg into the water. Bring the water temperature up slightly to maintain a low boil. Using a large slotted spoon, very carefully lift each egg off the bottom of the pot to ensure it doesn't stick. Cook the eggs approximately 4 minutes for a soft-medium poach or until they are done to your preference—remember that the eggs will continue to cook once they are removed from the heat.

Using a slotted spoon, remove each egg from the pot and place on top of the bagel halves. Garnish each with about ½ cup (125 mL) of warm Hollandaise Sauce and season with sea salt and black pepper. Serve immediately.

Serves 2

2 bagels or English muffins, sliced
¼ cup (60 mL) Smoked Salmon Terrine (page 24)
1 cup (250 mL) fresh crabmeat
1 ripe avocado, sliced
1 Tbsp (15 mL) white wine vinegar or apple cider vinegar
4 eggs
2 cups (500 mL) Hollandaise Sauce (page 150)
Sea salt, to taste
Freshly cracked black pepper, to taste

Warm Crab and Artichoke Dip

For a gluten-free option, serve this delicious dip with crisp apple slices or a variety of vegetables—both offer a nice, cool crunch to go with the warm and gooey yumminess of the dip.

Preheat the oven to 350°F (180°C). Whisk together the cream cheese and Greek yogurt. Add the garlic, scallions, and Dijon mustard. Fold in the artichoke hearts, crab-meat, and 1 cup (250 mL) of the cheese, being careful to leave some larger crab chunks. Transfer to a high-sided, oven-proof serving dish and sprinkle the remaining ¼ cup (60 mL) of cheese on top. Bake 25 to 30 minutes or until the dip is bubbling and golden brown.

Serve warm with fresh French bread, grilled baguette, or your favourite tortilla chips.

Serves 6 to 8

1 package (250 g) cream cheese, room temperature

⅔ cup (165 mL) plain Greek yogurt

1 clove of garlic, minced

¼ cup (60 mL) finely chopped scallions

1 Tbsp (15 mL) Dijon mustard

6 oz (170 g) jar of artichoke hearts, drained and chopped

1 lb (450 g) cooked crabmeat

1¼ cup (310 mL) shredded cheese (Parmesan, asiago, and cheddar), divided

Crab and Pancetta Hasselback Potatoes

Hasselback potatoes are basically a blank canvas that can be stuffed with whatever suits your fancy. Try using baby shrimp or candied salmon instead of or along with the crabmeat.

Preheat the oven to 425°F (220°C).

Make ⅛-inch-thick (0.3 cm) slices in each potato, not slicing all the way through the bottom and stopping about ⅛ inch from the ends. Place the potatoes on a baking sheet lined with parchment paper. Brush each with olive oil. Season with sea salt and black pepper. Place in the oven and cook 30 to 40 minutes, until the potato is *al dente* and the slices become flexible enough to spread apart and stuff.

In a bowl, combine the crabmeat, pancetta, thyme, and smoked paprika.

Remove baking sheet from the oven. Stuff the slices with the crab/pancetta mixture and top with shredded cheese. Return to the oven and cook another 15 to 20 minutes or until the cheese has melted and is bubbly.

To serve, top each potato with half of the sour cream and half of the scallion slices.

Serves 2 to 4

2 large russet potatoes, scrubbed
2 Tbsp (30 mL) olive oil
½ tsp (2.5 mL) sea salt
¼ tsp (1 mL) freshly cracked black pepper
½ lb (225 g) cooked crabmeat
¼ lb (110 g) pancetta, browned
1 tsp (5 mL) fresh thyme leaves
½ tsp (2.5 mL) smoked paprika
1½ cup (375 mL) shredded cheese, sharp cheddar and mozzarella
¼ cup (60 mL) sour cream
1 scallion, thinly sliced

Dungeness Crab Cakes with Harissa Aioli

These crab cakes are perfect for passing around as hors d'oeuvres at a party and can be fully made up to a day in advance. Make 12 bite-sized cakes instead of 6 lunchtime servings, and pop them in a 375°F (190°C) degree oven for 10 minutes to re-crisp and heat through before serving. Not a fan of harissa? Try them with Tartar Sauce (page 148) or Chipotle Peach Salsa (page 64).

In a frying pan over medium-high heat, place the diced onion and 2 Tbsp (30 mL) of the vegetable oil. Fry, stirring infrequently so that the onion begins to caramelize but does not burn, approximately 5 minutes. Reduce the heat and continue to fry until the onion is deep gold in colour. Remove from heat and let cool.

In a bowl, mix together the crabmeat, caramelized onion, chives, black pepper, smoked paprika, lemon zest, lemon juice, and sea salt. Lightly beat 3 of the eggs and add to the crab mixture along with ¾ cup of panko. Mix all together and use hands to form into 6 cakes. Place on a parchment-lined baking sheet and chill in the freezer for 30 minutes to 1 hour.

In a separate bowl, beat the remaining 2 eggs with water. Place the remaining 1 cup (250 mL) of panko in another bowl. Dip each crab cake first in the egg mixture and then in the panko. Be sure to coat the edges and both sides of the cakes with each.

Heat the remaining oil in a large, flat-bottomed frying pan over medium-low heat. Cook the crab cakes 4 minutes per side or until crispy and golden brown. Serve warm with Harissa Aioli (page 149).

Serves 6

1 medium onion, diced
⅓ cup (80 mL) vegetable oil, divided
1½ lb (680 g) Dungeness crabmeat, well drained and all shells removed
2 Tbsp (30 mL) finely chopped fresh chives
2 tsp (10 mL) freshly cracked black pepper (for heat, optional)
2 tsp (10 mL) smoked paprika
2 tsp (10 mL) freshly grated lemon zest
2 tsp (10 mL) freshly squeezed lemon juice
1 tsp (5 mL) sea salt
5 large eggs, divided
1 Tbsp (15 mL) water
1¾ cup (415 mL) panko-style bread crumbs, divided
Harissa Aioli (page 149)

Beach-Boiled Crab with Herb Butter

These simply cooked crabs are equally delicious served alongside Aioli (page 149) or, for lighter fare, Champagne Mignonette (page 148). If you have leftover crabmeat, it can be used in the Crab and Pancetta Hasselback Potatoes (page 101) or the Dungeness Crab Cakes with Harissa Aioli (page 102). If you don't have access to an extra-large pot or cleaning a crab seems too daunting, have your fishmonger clean and halve live crabs for you; just be sure to cook them as soon as possible afterward. To extract the meat from the crabs, be sure to set out seafood "crackers" and long seafood forks: these make accessing the delectable meat a lot easier.

Estimate your cooking time by calculating the average weight of each crab: take the total weight of the crabs and divide by 2. Use the average weight to estimate your total cooking time by assuming 6 to 7 minutes per 1 lb. For example, if the total weight is 6 lbs, divide by 2 for an average of 3 lbs × 6 to 7 minutes and a total of 18 to 21 minutes of steam time.

Add enough water (sea water is best) to fill ⅔ of an oversize stock pot or large canning pot and bring the water to a rolling boil. Place the live crabs inside and cover with a tight-fitting lid. After cooking for the length of time you calculated, cool the crabs (dump them into the cool sea if you're lucky enough to be on a beach, or place them in a colander in the sink and run cool water over them for 5 to 6 minutes). Once they've cooled, give them a quick clean (page 96) and cut them in half.

While the crabs are cooling, melt the butter in a saucepan over medium-low heat. Reduce the heat to low and heat another 10 minutes, skim away the foam, and remove any white solids that form in the bottom of the pan. Add the herbs and lower the heat to the lowest setting. Keep warm until ready to use. To serve, add a pinch of *fleur de sel* to each of 4 ramekins and pour the warmed herb butter on top.

Serve crab halves with lemon wedges and ¼ cup (60 mL) of the herb butter dipping sauce per person.

Serves 4

2 live Dungeness crabs
1 cup (250 mL) unsalted butter
2 Tbsp (30 mL) finely chopped fresh parsley
2 Tbsp (30 mL) finely chopped fresh thyme
2 Tbsp (30 mL) finely chopped fresh tarragon
2 Tbsp (30 mL) finely chopped fresh chives
4 pinches *fleur de sel* or other high-quality flake sea salt
1 lemon cut into 8 wedges

Barbecued Dungeness Crab with Lemon Aioli

Crab responds wonderfully to different-flavoured aiolis, so feel free to switch it up. Try it with Herb Aioli (page 149), or if you're looking for a little spice, try the sriracha or chipotle version (page 149).

〜〜〜〜〜〜〜〜〜〜〜〜〜〜〜〜〜〜〜〜〜〜〜〜〜〜〜〜〜〜〜〜

Have your fishmonger split and clean the crabs for you; cook them as quickly as possible afterward.

Preheat the barbecue. Wrap each crab individually in foil, carefully sealing it. Place on the grill and cover. Cook until tender, 8 to 10 minutes, flipping halfway through. Take the crabs off the grill, remove from the foil, and serve with Lemon Aioli (page 149).

Serves 4

4 large Dungeness crabs
1 cup (250 mL) Lemon Aioli (page 149)

Tofino Beach Party Boil

This is the ultimate party food, perfect for gatherings with friends and family on the West Coast's gorgeous beaches. As we often have fire bans in the summer, portable propane cookers meant for larger pots are a perfect hot-weather heat source. If you're on the beach, try making this recipe using available sea water for an extra kick of flavour.

Place a large pot of water on an outdoor cooker or over medium-high heat indoors. Add the seafood seasoning ingredients and bring to a boil. Add potatoes and chorizo, and cook about 10 minutes. Add the corn, the onions, and crab, then cook another 5 minutes. Add the shrimp when everything else is almost done, and cook another 3 or 4 minutes. Drain the water and pour the contents out onto a table covered with newspaper. Serve with Classic Cocktail Sauce, Aioli, and an assortment of hot sauces.

Serves 12 to 16

Seafood Seasoning
6 cloves of garlic, peeled
5 bay leaves
5 whole cloves
2 Tbsp (30 mL) celery seeds
2 Tbsp (30 mL) sea salt
1 Tbsp (15 mL) freshly ground
   black pepper
1 Tbsp (15 mL) red pepper flakes
1 Tbsp (15 mL) smoked paprika
2 tsp (10 mL) dry English mustard
Pinch of nutmeg
Pinch of ground cinnamon

Boil
5 lbs (2.25 kg) new potatoes
3 lbs (1.36 kg) cooked and dried
   chorizo
8 ears of fresh corn, husks and silks
   removed, cut in half
2 golden onions, peeled and quartered
5 lbs (2.25 kg) whole crab, broken into
   pieces
4 lbs (1.8 kg) fresh shrimp, shells on,
   heads and tails intact
Classic Cocktail Sauce (page 148)
Aioli (page 149)

FRUITS de MER:

Eat as the French Do

The French call the succulent, sweet, and juicy mollusc class of shellfish (along with crustaceans) *fruits de mer*, the fruits of the sea, and it's easy to see why. To us, no other seafood has the more-ishness of these gorgeous little ocean darlings, and the cold waters around BC's West Coast produce some of the best in the world. We find they take beautifully to any sauce they're introduced to, and of course, when it comes to oysters, we like them straight up—fresh and raw and on the half shell.

Regional breeds of molluscs are, if you'll pardon the pun, making waves on the international scene right now: Salt Spring Island mussels are sought-after for their generous size and delicious, creamy meat; Fanny Bay and Denman Island oysters make the menus of top oyster bars throughout the Pacific Northwest; and Qualicum Beach clams are a go-to for skillet clams and West Coast clam chowders alike.

Prepping them is fairly easy: most just need a scrub, and if your fishmonger hasn't debearded your mussels for you, a simple tug of the "beard" under warm water should release it fairly easily. The most important thing when cooking clams, oysters, scallops, and mussels is making sure they're *alive* when you get them and keeping them alive. Do not, I repeat, *do not* seal them in a plastic bag, as they will suffocate quickly, but if kept cold in an open bag they should last for a day or two in the fridge if necessary. Once steamed or cooked in a dish, discard any that do not open, as this is an indication that they were dead before cooking.

One of the nicest things about the *fruits de mer* is that their environmental impact is kept to a minimum. Yes, unless you're down on the beach collecting them yourself, most of them are farmed, but because they eat by filtering plankton from the water, no additional feed, antibiotics, or chemicals are needed for raising them. The choice between on-bottom farming and off-bottom aquaculture, where the mussels or oysters are invited to grow on suspended platforms or chains, is one to consider, but both aim for minimal impact on the ocean floor. We choose off-bottom when possible, as dredging can do some damage, however minimal. Clams and scallops that are hand-collected may be slightly more expensive, but the cost compared to the damage of dredging is worthwhile, in our opinion.

Oysters
***

Scallops
***

Mussels
✳ ✳ ✳

Clams
✳ ✳ ✳

OYSTERS

An old wives' tale tells us that we should only eat oysters in the months whose names contain an R—thus, September through April is safe for indulging our mollusc cravings. The truth, however, is that shellfish toxicity levels are closely monitored year-round by official agencies, and beds are shut down anytime algae levels become dangerous for human consumption or when the oysters are in a spawning cycle. Your best and safest bet—especially if you love your oysters raw—is to ask your local supplier, fishmonger, or Fisheries and Oceans Canada if it's safe to collect and eat from your local beds. Most of the oysters we buy commercially are farmed and are reared with the highest eco-standards in mind.

The oysters here on the West Coast come in a variety of sizes and textures. From the large and gloriously salty Fanny Bay oysters to the tiny and exquisitely creamy Kusshi oysters, the range available makes BC an oyster lover's paradise. So how do you like them? Raw, smoked, baked, or fried, we love them! If you're eating them raw, they'll be alive when you bring them home. Don't be daunted by the idea of shucking—it's easier than you think.

How to Shuck an Oyster

Getting an oyster to open doesn't have to be a difficult task. With a little patience and these handy tips, you'll be a pro in no time.

1. **Always, always use the freshest of live oysters**. Never close them in a plastic bag, as they can suffocate quite quickly.
2. **Use a good shucker**. Your knife doesn't need to be super sharp, but a blade with a point and a sturdy handle will make your work much easier.
3. **A tea towel helps**. Wrapping the oyster in a tea towel will save your hands from the sharp shells as well as catch the liquid that inevitably pours out once the oyster opens.
4. **Find the sweet spot**. Insert the knife point slowly into the edge of the hinge, where the top and bottom shells meet. Don't come at it straight from the back: coming from the side of the hinge will allow you to have maximum leverage without cracking the shell.
5. **Go slowly**. It doesn't take a lot of force to get an oyster open, and chances are, if you push too hard you'll not only tear apart the delicate oyster meat inside, you'll also go right through the shell and into your hand. This is a case of slow and steady wins the fight.
6. **Cut the oyster from its shell**. Once the shell opens, run the blade gently under the oyster to release the meat from the "foot." That way, it'll slide off the shell beautifully, instead of you having to rip it off with your teeth.

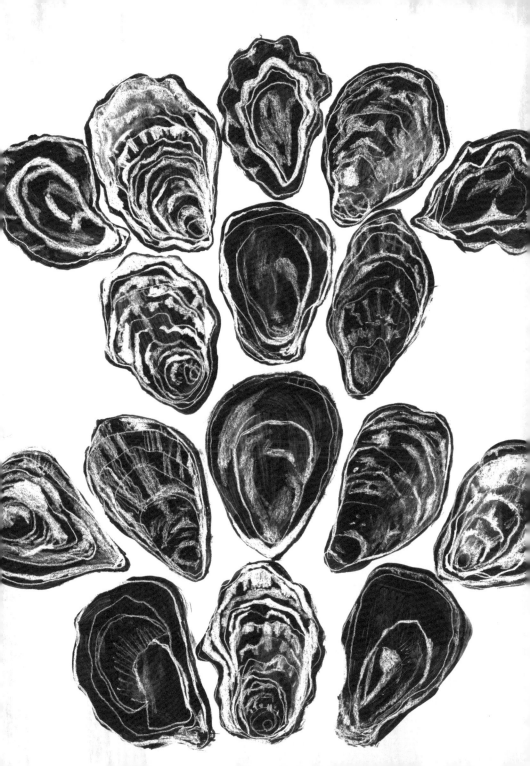

Oysters on the Half Shell with Champagne Mignonette

This is the simplest of recipes. The key is the freshness of the oysters: be sure they're alive when they're shucked and keep them as cold as possible throughout. If you prefer a stronger-flavoured mignonette, try swapping the champagne vinegar for raspberry vinegar or sherry vinegar.

Prepare the Champagne Mignonette at least an hour ahead and as far in advance as the day before.

When you're ready to serve them, place the shucked oysters on a bed of ice and serve with Champagne Mignonette, horseradish, and lemon wedges.

Serves 4

Champagne Mignonette (page 148)

12 shucked fresh, live oysters, such as Fanny Bay or Kusshi

2 Tbsp (30 mL) freshly grated horseradish

1 lemon cut into 12 thin wedges

Fried Oyster Po' Boy with Smoky Chipotle Aioli

The chipotle in this recipe gives the sandwiches a bit of a kick. We've aimed for a medium spice level; adjust to your comfort level. Don't like spice at all? This sandwich is traditionally served with a Rémoulade (page 149), perfect for pickle lovers everywhere.

Pat the water off the oysters with a paper towel and place them in a small non-reactive bowl. Cover them with the buttermilk and let rest for 10 to 15 minutes.

In a medium bowl, whisk together the eggs, milk, and cayenne pepper. Place the cornmeal, flour, baking powder, black pepper, and sea salt in another bowl and mix well.

Using a large heavy-bottomed pot, add enough oil to fill it 2 inches deep. Heat until a candy/deep-fry thermometer reads 360°F (180°C).

Preheat the oven to 170°F (75°C).

One by one, lift the oysters from the buttermilk using a slotted spoon. Dip each oyster into the egg mixture and then the cornmeal mixture. Toss to coat well. Spread out the coated oysters on a parchment-paper-lined baking sheet and working in batches, carefully drop them into the oil. Fry until golden brown and cooked through, approximately 3 minutes. Drain on a paper towel; keep warm in the oven until ready to serve.

Slice the hoagie buns horizontally and toast lightly in the toaster. Spread a generous amount of Smoky Chipotle Aioli on each half, layer the butter lettuce and sliced tomato inside, and fill with oysters. Serve with lemon wedges.

Serves 4

- 2 lb (900 g) freshly shucked oysters
- 1 cup (250 mL) buttermilk
- 2 eggs
- 2 Tbsp (30 mL) milk
- 1 tsp (5 mL) cayenne pepper
- ¾ cup (185 mL) cornmeal
- ¾ cup (185 mL) all-purpose flour
- 2 tsp (10 mL) baking powder
- Pinch of freshly ground black pepper
- Pinch of sea salt
- Vegetable oil, for frying
- 4 hoagie buns
- 1 cup (250 mL) Smoky Chipotle Aioli (page 149)
- 8 butter lettuce leaves
- 2 medium-size ripe tomatoes, cut into ¼-inch (0.5 cm) slices
- 1 lemon cut into quarters

Cheesy Baked Oysters

This delicious cheesy topping will work with any mollusc: scallops, clams, even mussels. Serve with a dark porter or rich stout for the ultimate seafood comfort meal.

Preheat the oven to 400°F (200°C).

In a medium-sized bowl, combine the cheeses, bread crumbs, parsley, and thyme. Set aside.

In a small saucepan, melt the butter over medium heat. Add the lemon zest, lemon juice, hot sauce, garlic, and Worcestershire sauce, stirring to combine. Let cool slightly. Once cooled, fold the melted butter mixture into the cheese mixture and combine well.

Place the oysters on the half shell on a baking sheet, making sure they are stable—a layer of salt on the baking sheet can help to hold them in position while in the oven. Top each oyster with an equal amount of the cheese and butter mixture. Bake in the oven for 8 to 10 minutes, or until the topping is golden and bubbly. Serve 3 oysters per person alongside crusty bread.

Serves 4

¼ cup (60 mL) grated asiago cheese
¼ cup (60 mL) grated Monterey Jack cheese
¼ cup (60 mL) grated fontina cheese
¼ cup (60 mL) dried bread crumbs
½ cup (125 mL) chopped parsley
2 Tbsp (30 mL) fresh thyme leaves
½ cup (125 mL) butter
1 tsp (5 mL) freshly grated lemon zest
2 Tbsp (30 mL) freshly squeezed lemon juice
2 Tbsp (30 mL) hot sauce
2 garlic cloves, minced
⅓ cup (80 mL) Worcestershire sauce
12 Fanny Bay or other medium-sized oysters, shucked, and on the half shell
Crusty loaf of bread or baguette

Smoked Oyster Pot Pie

This is a versatile pot pie recipe that works well with salmon, halibut, or even shrimp or prawns substituted for the oysters.

Preheat the oven to 400°F (200°C). Place the oysters in a bowl with ⅓ cup (80 mL) of the oyster liquor they've emitted.

In a large pot or Dutch oven, cook the bacon over medium heat until crispy and golden brown—about 6 to 7 minutes. Remove the bacon from the pot.

Deglaze the pot by pouring the white wine and lemon juice in and stirring to scrape up any bacon bits that come loose from the bottom. Add the butter, onion, carrots, and celery, and sauté 3 to 4 minutes. Add the garlic and cook 1 more minute. Stirring constantly, add the flour and cook for an additional 2 to 3 minutes or until the flour begins to bubble. Continuing to stir, slowly add the fish stock. Stir in the cream and reserved oyster liquor. Add the seafood seasoning, sea salt, black pepper, and nutmeg. Stirring constantly, cook 3 to 4 more minutes or until the mixture thickens—it should be the consistency of a thick pancake batter.

Remove the pot from the heat and stir in the smoked oysters and bacon. Spoon the mixture into 6 lightly greased 12 oz (340 g) ramekins. Roll out the pastry sheets, cut into circles that are slightly larger than the ramekins, and place each circle over top of the filling in each ramekin. Whisk together the egg and water. Using a pastry brush, spread the mixture over the pastry.

Bake at 400°F (200°C) on the lower rack of the oven for 30 to 35 minutes or until browned and bubbly. Let stand for 15 minutes before serving.

Serves 6

1 cup (250 mL) smoked oysters, cut into ½-inch (1 cm) chunks
4 thick bacon slices, cut into medium-sized chunks
¼ cup (60 mL) white wine
2 Tbsp (30 mL) freshly squeezed lemon juice
3 Tbsp (45 mL) butter
1 medium yellow onion, diced
½ cup (125 mL) diced carrots
½ cup (125 mL) diced celery
1 garlic clove, minced
¼ cup (60 mL) all-purpose flour
¾ cup (185 mL) Fish Stock (page 152)
¾ cup (185 mL) heavy cream
2 tsp (10 mL) Seafood Seasoning (page 152) or Old Bay
Pinch of sea salt
1 tsp (5 mL) freshly ground black pepper
½ tsp (2.5 mL) freshly grated nutmeg
1 lb (450 g) package of puff pastry
1 egg
1 TB (15 mL) water

SCALLOPS

One of the most elegant types of shellfish, scallops are often associated with fine dining, but that doesn't have to be the case. No seafood is easier to cook, and the addition of scallops to pasta or risotto, or even as a side dish to beautifully grilled meat can take your home cooking from everyday to extraordinary with very little effort on your part. All they need are a very hot skillet and a simple 1-to-2-minute sear per side. Be sure not to overcook—you want them to be just warmed through at the centre, much like a medium-rare steak.

There are a few varieties of scallops available here on the West Coast, but we love Qualicum Beach scallops, which are sustainably farmed and cause none of the same disturbance to the ocean floor as traditional trawling, nor any bycatch, as they are hand-collected. You may be wary of "farmed" seafood, but because the scallops grow suspended, feed on wild plankton, and offer ecosystem benefits, they're more of an organic crop than your typical fish-farm catch.

Prawn and Scallop Ceviche

If your fishmonger has access to unspoiled scallop shells, they make the most beautiful serving vessels for this elegant dish.

In a large glass bowl, combine the prawns, scallops, lemon juice, lime juice, orange juice, red onion, and cucumber. Cover and chill in the refrigerator for 3 hours or until the seafood turns opaque, indicating that it has cured. Add the tomatoes, cilantro, chili, sea salt, and black pepper to the prawn and scallop mixture and stir to combine.

Serves 4

1 lb (450 g) spot prawns, de-headed, peeled, deveined, tails removed, and quartered
1 lb (450 g) scallops, quartered
¼ cup (60 mL) freshly squeezed lemon juice
¼ cup (60 mL) freshly squeezed lime juice
¼ cup (60 mL) freshly squeezed orange juice
¼ cup (60 mL) finely chopped red onion
½ cup (125 mL) diced cucumber
1 cup (250 mL) diced tomatoes
¼ cup (60 mL) chopped cilantro
1 tsp (5 mL) finely chopped fresh chili
½ tsp (2.5 mL) sea salt
½ tsp (2.5 mL) freshly cracked black pepper

Pancetta-Wrapped Scallops with Lemon Butter Sauce

If you don't have easy access to proper pancetta, a thin, streaky bacon will work just as well.

Preheat the oven's broiler.

Season the scallops with sea salt and black pepper. Wrap a slice of pancetta around each scallop and fasten with a toothpick. Place scallops on a parchment-paper-lined baking sheet. Broil for 1 to 2 minutes per side, until pancetta is sizzling.

Melt the butter in a small pot over low heat. Add the lemon juice, lemon zest, Worcestershire sauce, and parsley and mix to combine. Season to taste with sea salt and black pepper. Transfer to 4 small dipping bowls and serve alongside the pancetta-wrapped scallops.

Serves 4

12 large scallops
Sea salt and freshly cracked black pepper, to taste
6 thin slices of pancetta, halved lengthwise
¼ cup (60 mL) butter
¼ cup (60 mL) freshly squeezed lemon juice
½ tsp (2.5 mL) freshly grated lemon zest
1 tsp (5 mL) Worcestershire sauce
1 Tbsp (15 mL) finely chopped parsley

Seared Scallop and Orzo Salad

The salad base of this recipe is wonderful with myriad types of seafood. Try it with seared spot prawns or freshly cooked crabmeat; even a flaked salmon fillet is nice with it.

Fill a medium saucepan with water and a pinch of sea salt; bring to a boil and add the orzo. Cook per package instructions. Drain and rinse with warm water. Transfer to a large bowl and add 4 Tbsp (60 mL) of the olive oil, the lemon zest and juice, and the black pepper. Set aside.

In a large skillet over medium heat, add the butter. Once melted, add the diced onion and stir to coat well with the butter. Fry the onions for 8 to 10 minutes—do not over-stir. The onions are done when they are deep golden in colour; add to the orzo.

Pat the scallops dry and lightly season with sea salt. Heat the remaining 2 Tbsp (30 mL) of olive oil in a large frying pan over medium-high heat. Once the oil is heated, sear one side of the scallops for 1 to 2 minutes. Flip carefully and repeat on the other side. The scallops should be a deep golden brown on both sides and slightly soft to the touch; they continue to cook for a few minutes once removed from the heat, so be sure not to overcook. Remove the scallops and add the white wine to the pan. Cook for 1 minute to loosen any bits stuck to the bottom. Pour the pan juices over the orzo and add the scallops, spinach, tomatoes, and tarragon. Toss to combine and serve immediately.

Serves 4

Pinch of sea salt
2 cups (500 mL) orzo
6 Tbsp (90 mL) olive oil,
 divided
Freshly grated zest and
 freshly squeezed juice
 of 1 lemon
1 tsp (5 mL) freshly cracked
 black pepper, or to taste
2 Tbsp (30 mL) unsalted
 butter
1 small onion, diced small
1 pound (450 g) medium
 scallops, "foot" muscles
 removed
½ cup (125 mL) dry
 white wine
2 cups (500 mL) baby
 spinach
1 cup (250 mL) halved
 cherry tomatoes
¼ cup (60 mL) chopped
 fresh tarragon

Brown Butter Scallops with Parmesan Risotto

A lot of stirring is involved in cooking risotto, so have everything ready to go before starting: this isn't the kind of dish you can walk away from. Don't be daunted, though—it's much easier than most believe, and the results are absolutely worth it. Try adding other flavours and ingredients as the seasons allow: leeks, fresh green peas, mint, tarragon, and thyme are all great accompaniments to the rich butteriness of the scallops.

In a medium saucepan, heat the olive oil over medium-high heat until hot. Reduce the heat to medium and add the diced onions. Cook 5 minutes, stirring constantly, until the onions become translucent. Add the rice and cook while stirring an additional 3 to 4 minutes. Add 3 Tbsp (45 mL) of butter and cook another 3 minutes while stirring constantly.

Add the wine, lemon juice, and lemon zest, and continue to stir. Once the liquid has been absorbed, add the warm stock in 1 cup (250 mL) increments, stirring constantly. Cook until each cup has been absorbed before adding the next. This should take about 20 to 25 minutes, and the rice will be *al dente* when ready. Add the remaining 3 Tbsp (45 mL) butter and the Parmigiano-Reggiano, mix, and keep warm until serving. If the rice becomes too sticky for serving, add an additional 1 cup (250 mL) of warm stock just before plating: the risotto should be loose, not gloopy.

Pat the scallops dry with a paper towel and lightly season with sea salt and black pepper. Working quickly, add the 6 Tbsp (90 mL) of butter to a skillet over medium heat. While stirring, melt the butter and continue to cook another 2 to 3 minutes. As the butter starts to turn golden, add the scallops and increase the heat to medium-high.

Sear one side of the scallops for 1 to 2 minutes in the butter while spooning the butter over top. Flip carefully and repeat on the other side. Scallops should be a deep golden brown on both sides and slightly soft to the touch—they

Serves 4

Risotto
2 Tbsp (30 mL) olive oil
1 medium onion, diced small
3 cups (750 mL) uncooked Arborio or Carnaroli rice
6 Tbsp (90 mL) unsalted butter, divided in half
1½ cups (375 mL) white wine
2 Tbsp (30 mL) freshly squeezed lemon juice
Freshly grated zest of 1 lemon
10 to 12 cups (2.5 L to 3 L) warm chicken stock or vegetable stock
2 cups (500 mL) grated Parmigiano-Reggiano cheese, plus more for topping

continue to cook for a few minutes once removed from the heat, so be sure not to overcook. Remove them from the heat and plate immediately.

Divide the risotto between the plates and top with additional Parmigiano-Reggiano. Place the scallops on top of the risotto and drizzle the whole dish with browned butter from the skillet.

Scallops

16 to 20 fresh scallops

6 Tbsp (90 mL) unsalted
   butter

Sea salt and freshly cracked
   black pepper to taste

MUSSELS

The number one rule when cooking any member of the mollusc family—e.g., mussels, oysters, and clams—is that unless they're canned or smoked, they should be alive when cooked. You'll know they're done when their shells open widely, and any that don't open should be discarded immediately. There's nothing simpler than a little steam, a little heat, a splash of wine in a hot pan for a moment or two, and *voilà!* Pure creamy, briny goodness. Mussels don't require much preparation, but some need to be "debearded" to make them nicer to eat: you'll notice they have a rough, hairy ridge around the edge of their shells. Simply give a good tug under some water and it will come away, or ask your fishmonger if they can do it for you.

Aurelia is French and was raised eating the *moules* her father cooked in the most traditional of ways. Here, she's given us three versions that should satisfy a variety of tastes. Be sure to serve them with lots of crusty bread, as you'll want to soak up every drop of the delicious steaming broths.

Salt Spring Island Mussels 3 Ways

Aurelia's father is the king of cooking mussels, especially in the classic French method. Here are three variations to choose from depending on your culinary mood: one savoury, one spicy, one traditional.

Serves 4

Tomato Garlic Mussels

In a large stock pot, heat the olive oil over medium heat. Add the garlic and cook 1 minute until just golden. Add wine, tomatoes, and red pepper flakes. Bring to a boil. Add the mussels and cover. Cook 5 minutes or until they open.

Transfer mussels to a serving bowl, discarding any that are unopened. Garnish with basil leaves and serve immediately.

1 Tbsp (15 mL) olive oil
3 cloves of garlic, sliced finely
1 cup (250 mL) dry white wine
6 Italian plum tomatoes, cored and diced
½ tsp (2.5 mL) red pepper flakes (optional)
4 lb (2 kg) fresh mussels, scrubbed and debearded
1 Tbsp (15 mL) finely chopped fresh basil leaves

Thai Curry Mussels

In a large pot, combine the coconut milk, lime juice, white wine, curry paste, garlic, fish sauce, and coconut sugar, and bring to a boil. Stir to dissolve the curry paste and sugar. Add the mussels, stir, and cover. Cook 5 to 8 minutes, until the mussels open.

Remove from the heat and stir in 1 cup (250 mL) chopped cilantro. Transfer to 4 serving bowls. Garnish with remaining ½ cup (250 mL) chopped cilantro.

13 oz (400 mL) can unsweetened coconut milk
½ cup (125 mL) freshly squeezed lime juice
½ cup (125 mL) dry white wine
1 Tbsp (15 mL) red or green Thai curry paste
1 garlic clove, minced
2 tsp (10 mL) fish sauce
2 tsp (10 mL) coconut sugar (white or brown sugar as a substitute)
4 lb (2 kg) fresh mussels, scrubbed and debearded
1½ cups (375 mL) chopped cilantro

Classic French Mussels

In a heavy stock pot over medium heat, melt the butter. Add the shallots and cook, stirring often, until translucent; do not brown. Add the wine and cream and bring to a boil.

Add the mussels and cover. Cook 5 minutes, or until they open. Toss the mussels with ⅔ cup (165 mL) of parsley and divide between four bowls, discarding any that are unopened.

To serve, garnish with the remaining parsley and add salt and pepper to taste.

1 Tbsp (15 mL) butter
1 shallot, sliced finely
2 cups (500 mL) oaked white wine
½ cup (125 mL) heavy cream
4 lb (2 kg) mussels, scrubbed and debearded
1 cup (250 mL) chopped parsley
Flaked sea salt such as *fleur de sel*
Freshly cracked black pepper

One Pot Cioppino

We've used the classic fruits de mer *in this dish, but any hearty white fish, such as halibut or sablefish, would be a nice addition.*

In a large pot, heat the oil and onions and cook until soft. Add the garlic, thyme, oregano, and red pepper flakes, and cook another minute. Add the crushed tomatoes and their juice, white wine, water, bay leaves, and honey. Bring to a boil, then simmer for 10 minutes.

Add the mussels and clams and cover. Simmer on low for 10 minutes. Add the shrimp, cover, and simmer for 2 to 3 minutes. Remove from heat and discard any unopened mussels or clams.

Garnish with parsley and serve.

Serves 4 to 6

¼ cup (60 mL) olive oil
1 medium onion, chopped
2 garlic cloves, minced
2 tsp (10 mL) fresh thyme
2 tsp (10 mL) dried oregano
½ tsp (2.5 mL) red pepper flakes
28 oz (800 g) can crushed tomatoes, with juice
1 cup (250 mL) dry white wine
1 cup (250 mL) water
2 dried bay leaves
1 tsp (5 mL) honey
1 lb (450 g) mussels, scrubbed and debearded
1 lb (450 g) clams, scrubbed
1 lb (450 g) shrimp, de-headed, peeled, deveined, and tails on
½ cup (125 mL) coarsely chopped parsley

Pacific Pasta Pescatore

This quick and easy pasta dish is perfect for mid-week meals. Serve with good, crusty bread—you won't want to miss any flavours at the bottom of the bowl!

Cook pasta per package instructions. Set aside.

In a large pot, heat the oil and onion. Cook until the onions are translucent, about 5 to 8 minutes. Add the garlic, stir, and cook another 2 minutes. Add the white wine and fish stock, and bring to a boil. Add the cherry tomatoes, capers, and seafood; stir and cover. Simmer on low heat for 6 to 8 minutes. Season with sea salt and black pepper. Serve with the pasta.

Serves 4

1 lb (450 g) pasta of your choice, such as *creste di gallo* or linguine
2 Tbsp (30 mL) olive oil
⅓ cup (80 mL) diced onion
2 garlic cloves, minced
½ cup (125 mL) dry white wine
1½ cups (375 mL) Fish Stock (page 152)
1 pint (475 g) cherry tomatoes, halved
2 Tbsp capers
12 mussels, scrubbed and debearded
12 large shrimp, de-headed, peeled, deveined, and tails on
8 large scallops
½ tsp (2.5 mL) sea salt
¼ tsp (1 mL) freshly cracked black pepper

CLAMS

For me, there are few things more fun or nostalgic than digging for clams on a sandy beach. My summers were spent between Deep Bay and Qualicum Beach on Vancouver Island, where the local clams are prolific. Even if we weren't planning to eat them, we kids loved to dig them up and then watch them bury themselves in their sandy beds. Today I'm a great fan of clams in the kitchen—in chowder, pasta, and paella—or even tossed on the barbecue and then drizzled with garlic butter, clambake style. Much like their cousins the mussels, they are sustainably raised and need little more than some applied heat when cooking to make them spring open; any that don't should be thrown away.

If you're looking for a quick-and-easy yet delicious mid-week meal, our local Manila clams and any white wine are a match made in culinary heaven. There's just something about the fruitiness of a good sauvignon blanc and the briny sweetness of clams when served with a handful of fresh herbs and a chunk of French bread that screams both *comfort food* and *luxury cuisine*.

Skillet-Steamed Clams with White Wine

The quality of the wine makes a difference here. As well, different wines can be used to change the flavour profile of the dish: try a dry white for a crisper taste, or a good oaky chardonnay to give the clams some depth. Don't forget the crusty bread—you won't want to let those pan juices go to waste.

In a large skillet over medium heat, melt the butter and add the garlic, red pepper flakes, lemon zest, sea salt, and black pepper; sauté until the garlic becomes golden. Add the clams and toss quickly to coat with butter. Add the wine and cover with a lid to steam for about 2 minutes, or until most of the clams are open; discard any that remain closed.

To serve, squeeze the lemon juice over the clams and garnish with freshly chopped parsley. Serve with crusty bread.

Serves 4

½ cup (125 mL) unsalted butter
3 cloves garlic, minced
2 tsp (10 mL) red pepper flakes
1 tsp (5 mL) freshly grated lemon zest
Pinch of sea salt
Pinch of freshly cracked black pepper
2 lb (900 g) fresh clams, shells scrubbed
½ cup (125 mL) white wine
½ a lemon, for juicing
Freshly chopped parsley to garnish
Sliced loaf of crusty French-style bread

Easy Seafood Paella

Making paella in the traditional way is a long process that involves cooking with a specialized pan over an open flame; here, we've provided an easy version that can be done at home in a regular skillet. Be sure to include the saffron—it gives the paella its trademark colour and distinctive flavour.

In a large skillet, heat the olive oil. Add the chorizo and chicken chunks, and cook until well browned. Deglaze the skillet by adding the sherry, and stir to scrape off any bits from the bottom. Cook for a few minutes until the alcohol evaporates. Add the tomato paste and cook another minute. Add the crushed tomatoes and oregano. Bring to a boil and stir in the rice. Add 4 cups (1 L) chicken stock and the saffron. Stir gently and cover. Simmer for 10 to 15 minutes. Uncover and add the mussels and shrimp and a bit more stock if needed, then cover. Cook another 5 to 8 minutes or until the mussels have opened (discard any that haven't).

Serves 4 to 6

1 Tbsp (15 mL) olive oil
3 chorizo sausage links, crumbled
1 lb (450 g) chicken thighs, boneless, skinless, and cubed
⅓ cup (80 mL) sherry
2 Tbsp (30 mL) tomato paste
28 oz (800 g) can of crushed tomatoes, juice drained
1 tsp (5 mL) dried oregano
2 cups (500 mL) uncooked short-grain rice
5 cups (1.25 L) chicken stock, warmed and divided
Pinch of saffron threads
15 mussels, scrubbed and debearded
15 large shrimp, de-headed, peeled, deveined, tails on
½ cup (125 mL) chopped parsley
2 tsp (10 mL) paprika

West Coast Clam Chowder

If you prefer a creamy clam chowder to a traditional tomato base, follow the recipe for Pacific Seafood Chowder (page 48), substituting 1 lb (450 g) fresh clams, shells removed, for the fish and shellfish.

In a medium-sized saucepan, sauté the bacon over medium heat until it becomes a lovely golden brown; do not overcook. Remove from the pan and set aside. Add the olive oil to the pan as well as the onion, carrot, and celery and cook for 5 minutes or until tender. Add the garlic and cook another 1 or 2 minutes. Add the flour and stir; cook another 1 to 2 minutes. While whisking constantly, slowly pour in the Fish Stock and Clamato juice, and cook on medium-high for 5 minutes.

Turn the burner to medium-low heat and add the clams, tomatoes and their juice, tomato paste, bay leaf, fresh thyme, hot sauce, and Worcestershire sauce, stirring to combine. Add the potatoes and simmer an additional 15 to 20 minutes or until the potatoes are cooked through. Season with sea salt and black pepper to taste.

Serves 4 to 6

3 strips of bacon, diced
2 Tbsp (30 mL) olive oil
½ large yellow onion, diced
1 large carrot, diced
1 rib celery, diced
1 clove garlic, minced
2 tsp (10 mL) all-purpose flour
1½ cups (375 mL) Fish Stock (page 152)
1½ cups (375 mL) Clamato juice
¼ lb (113 g) fresh clams, shells removed
14 oz (398 mL) can diced tomatoes, with juice
2 Tbsp (30 mL) tomato paste
1 bay leaf
1 tsp (5 mL) fresh thyme leaves
2 tsp (10 mL) hot sauce, or to taste
1 tsp (5 mL) Worcestershire sauce
1½ cups (375 mL) Yukon Gold potatoes, cut into half-inch chunks
Sea salt and freshly cracked black pepper

ACCOMPANIMENTS

Champagne Mignonette

Combine all the ingredients in a Mason jar. Put on the lid and shake to combine. Chill in the refrigerator for at least 1 hour and as long as overnight. Will keep in the fridge up to 2 weeks.

½ cup (125 mL) champagne vinegar
3 Tbsp (45 mL) finely chopped shallots
3 Tbsp (45 mL) finely diced peeled cucumber
1 Tbsp (15 mL) sugar
½ tsp (2.5 mL) sea salt

Tartar Sauce

Combine all ingredients in a bowl, cover, and let chill for at least 30 minutes to marry the flavours. Will keep in the fridge for 2 to 3 days.

1 cup (250 mL) Aioli (page 149) or mayonnaise
¾ cup (185 mL) chopped sweet dill pickles
2 Tbsp (30 mL) finely chopped fresh dill
2 Tbsp (30 mL) finely chopped shallots
1 tsp (5 mL) freshly squeezed lemon juice
Pinch of sea salt
Pinch of freshly cracked black pepper

Classic Cocktail Sauce

Place all ingredients in a bowl and stir to combine well. Chill in the refrigerator at least 30 minutes before serving. Will keep in the fridge for 4 to 5 days.

1 cup (250 mL) ketchup
1 Tbsp (15 mL) freshly squeezed lemon juice
1 tsp (5 mL) freshly grated lemon zest
3 Tbsp (45 mL) freshly grated horseradish
2 tsp (10 mL) Worcestershire sauce
1 tsp (5 mL) Seafood Seasoning (page 152)

Aioli

Using a blender or food processor, mix the egg, garlic, and lemon juice together until well combined. With the machine running, add the sea salt and then slowly drizzle in the olive oil until the sauce emulsifies and thickens to a mayonnaise consistency. Will keep in the fridge 3 to 4 days.

Variations

Smoky Chipotle Aioli: 1 tsp (5 mL) finely chopped canned chipotle pepper with sauce, 1 finely minced clove of garlic, 1 tsp (5 mL) white wine vinegar

Lemon Aioli: 1 Tbsp (15 mL) freshly squeezed lemon juice, 1 tsp (5 mL) freshly grated lemon zest

Harissa Aioli: 2 to 3 tsp (10 to 15 mL) harissa olive oil or 1 tsp (5 mL) harissa paste

Sriracha Aioli: 1 to 2 Tbsp (15 to 30 mL) sriracha

Sesame Aioli: 1 tsp (5 mL) sesame oil, 2 tsp (10 mL) tahini

Herb Aioli: ¼ cup (60 mL) chopped fresh herbs of your choice

1 egg
3 cloves of garlic, minced
2 tsp (10 mL) freshly squeezed lemon juice
½ tsp (2.5 mL) sea salt
1 cup (250 mL) good-quality olive oil

Rémoulade

Place all ingredients in a blender or food processor and pulse until mostly smooth. Will keep in the fridge 3 to 4 days.

1 cup (250 mL) Aioli (page 149) or mayonnaise
¼ cup (60 mL) grainy mustard
1 Tbsp (15 mL) smoked paprika
2 tsp (10 mL) freshly grated horseradish
1 to 2 gherkin pickles
1 tsp (5 mL) hot sauce (preferably Louisiana style)
1 large garlic clove, minced

Hollandaise Sauce

3 egg yolks
1½ Tbsp (23 mL) freshly squeezed
lemon juice
½ cup (125 mL) unsalted butter,
melted
Pinch of sea salt
Pinch of freshly cracked black pepper

In the top of a double boiler or a small stainless-steel bowl, whisk the egg yolks and lemon juice together until the mixture begins to thicken significantly. Place the egg and lemon juice mixture on top of a double boiler base or a small pot of boiling water (the water should not touch the bottom of the bowl). While whisking constantly, slowly drizzle in the melted butter. The sauce should thicken again quite quickly. Remove from heat and whisk in the salt and pepper. Cover until ready to use. If you find the sauce has gotten too thick, add 1 tablespoon (15 mL) of hot water and stir to return to pouring consistency.

Variations
Dill Hollandaise Sauce: 2 Tbsp (30 mL) chopped
fresh dill
Chipotle Hollandaise Sauce: 1 to 2 tsp (5 to
10 mL) minced canned chipotle pepper
Cilantro Lime Hollandaise Sauce: 1 Tbsp
(15 mL) minced cilantro, 1 tsp (5 mL) freshly
squeezed lime juice, 1 tsp (5 mL) freshly grated
lime zest

Crème Fraîche

1 cup (250 mL) whipping cream
2 Tbsp (30 mL) buttermilk

Combine the whipping cream and buttermilk in a glass jar and cover with cheesecloth or waxed paper. Let sit at room temperature for 24 hours. Store in the fridge for up to a week.

Variations
Dill Crema: Add ¼ cup (60 mL) freshly chopped
dill and ¼ cup (60 mL) sour cream to Crème
Fraîche and chill in the fridge at least 15 minutes
to blend flavours.

Sweet and Sour Sauce

Combine all ingredients in a small pot and place over medium heat. Stir constantly until the sauce begins to thicken. Remove from stove and store in the refrigerator for up to a week.

½ cup (125 mL) pineapple juice
¼ cup (60 mL) packed brown sugar
3 Tbsp (45 mL) water
2 Tbsp (30 mL) vinegar
1 Tbsp (15 mL) soy sauce
1 Tbsp (15 mL) ketchup
1 Tbsp (15 mL) freshly grated ginger
5 tsp (25 mL) cornstarch

Spicy Sesame Dipping Sauce

Combine all ingredients in a bowl. Serve with dumplings.

¼ cup (60 mL) soy sauce
2 Tbsp (30 mL) fish sauce
2 Tbsp (30 mL) sesame oil
1 Tbsp (30 mL) sriracha or
  sambal oelek
1 Tbsp (15 mL) coconut sugar
  or white sugar
1 thinly sliced scallion

Sweet Chili Dipping Sauce

Combine all ingredients in a small pot and place over medium heat. Stir until the sugar dissolves and the sauce comes to a boil. Continue to boil until the liquid is reduced by half. Cool before serving.

½ cup (125 mL) brown sugar
1 cup (250 mL) water
¼ cup (60 mL) sambal oelek

Variations

Sweet Chili Lemon Sauce: Add 1 Tbsp (15 mL) cornstarch to ¼ cup (60 mL) freshly squeezed lemon juice. Add the lemon juice mixture to Sweet Chili Dipping Sauce at the end of the reduction process. Cook over medium heat for an additional 2 to 3 minutes or until the sauce loses its cloudiness due to the cornstarch. Cool before serving.

Seafood Seasoning

Combine all ingredients and grind in a spice grinder or mortar and pestle, and store in a sealed glass jar for up to 2 months.

5 bay leaves
5 cloves
2 Tbsp (30 mL) celery seeds
2 Tbsp (30 mL) sea salt
1 Tbsp (15 mL) freshly ground black pepper
1 Tbsp (15 mL) red pepper flakes
1 Tbsp (15 mL) smoked paprika
1 Tbsp (15 mL) garlic powder
2 tsp (10 mL) dry English mustard
Pinch of nutmeg
Pinch of ground cinnamon

Fish Stock

In the bottom of a 4-quart (4 L) stock pot, add the olive oil and sauté the onions, celery, and carrots until the vegetables begin to soften. Add the bones and continue to sauté another 5 to 6 minutes. Add the white wine and cook 2 to 3 minutes more.

Fill the pot two-thirds of the way with water and add the bay leaf, thyme, and peppercorns. Boil until the water has reduced by half, skimming off any foam along the way.

Strain through a cheesecloth-lined fine sieve. Season the stock with sea salt to taste. Use immediately or store in the refrigerator for up to 4 days. Stock will freeze well for 1 to 2 months.

If using fish heads as well, make sure the gills have been removed and that all the blood has been washed away.

2 Tbsp (30 mL) olive oil
1 medium onion, sliced
3 celery stalks, chopped
2 medium carrots, chopped
2 lbs (900 g) freshly cleaned fish bones from halibut and/or cod, cut into 2-inch pieces
½ cup (125 mL) white wine
1 dried bay leaf
8 sprigs fresh thyme
1 Tbsp (15 mL) black peppercorns
Sea salt to taste

ACKNOWLEDGMENTS

To my dearest husband, James: How can I ever begin to thank you? From the day you put the camera in my hands to the support and encouragement you've given along the way, none of this would be possible without your constant cheerleading. Go be awesome. Always.

To Aurelia, who makes food almost too pretty to eat, I never thought I'd find someone so easy to work with! Thank you for always being there, tirelessly, with laughter, Q-tips, and hot coffee along with your amazing eye for detail.

To Taryn and the TouchWood Editions team, thank you for believing in us and not being daunted by the tight timelines. This work poured out of us and you caught it, along with our dreams, and made it a reality.

To the Victoria crew at Finest at Sea, our heartfelt thanks for your incredible knowledge, beautiful selection, willingness to clean crabs, and constant vigilance regarding sustainability and good fishing practices.

To our friends and family members who ate, tested, and ate some more—cheers to full bellies and much laughter. A special thanks to Penny Hardie for making sure these recipes could translate overseas all the way to the Isle of Skye in Scotland, and to chef Maggie Aro, my oldest and dearest friend, for your invaluable input, observations, suggestions, and the best damn shrimp bisque that's ever been made! —Danielle

I would like to say a special thank you to Danielle, without whom this book would not have been possible. Her incredible talent and infinite knowledge have inspired my creativity. Her ability to bring the heart and soul of our seafood recipes from the plate to the pages is delectable. Working together, we get to share inspiring meals and a ton of laughter. How many can say they are so lucky? —Aurelia

ABOUT THE AUTHORS

Danielle [DL] Acken is a Canadian-born international food photographer and caterer who splits her time between London, UK, and her farm studio on BC's tranquil Salt Spring Island. When not in the kitchen or with camera in hand, she's travelling the world with her husband and their four adventurous children.

Aurelia Louvet is a dedicated home cook and food stylist based on Salt Spring Island. Having lived and eaten around the world, Aurelia's work delivers a unique combination of modern North American sensibility and classic European beauty.

Index

Edited by Amanda Growe
Designed and illustrated by Tree Abraham

LIBRARY AND ARCHIVES CANADA CATALOGUING IN PUBLICATION

Louvet, Aurelia, author
Off the hook : essential West Coast seafood recipes /
Aurelia Louvet and DL Acken.

Includes index.

Issued in print and electronic formats.
ISBN 978-1-77151-276-3 (softcover).—ISBN 978-1-77151-277-0 (HTML).—
ISBN 978-1-77151-278-7 (PDF)

1. Cooking (Seafood). 2. Cooking, Canadian--British Columbia style.
3. Cookbooks. I. Acken, DL (Danielle L.), photographer II. Title.

TX747.L688 2018   641.6'92   C2018-901897-6   C2018-901898-4

We acknowledge the financial support of the Government of Canada through the Canada Book Fund and the province of British Columbia through the Book Publishing Tax Credit.

Canadä

This book was produced using FSC®-certified, acid-free papers, processed chlorine-free and printed with soya-based inks.

Printed in Canada at Friesens

22 21 20 19 18   1 2 3 4 5